DOWNE HOUSE

'A MYSTERY AND A MIRACLE'

DOWNE HOUSE

'A MYSTERY AND A MIRACLE'

Edited by Val Horsler and Jennifer Kingsland

THIRD MILLENNIUM
PUBLISHING, LONDON

Copyright © Downe House School and
Third Millennium Publishing Limited

First published in 2006 by Third Millennium
Publishing Limited, a subsidiary of Third Millennium
Information Limited.

2–5 Benjamin Street
London
United Kingdom
EC1M 5QL
www.tmiltd.com

ISBN 10 : 1 903942 50 0
ISBN 13 : 978 1 903942 50 5

British Library Cataloguing in Publication Data

A CIP catalogue record for this book is available from the
British Library.

Edited by Val Horsler and Jennifer Kingsland
Designed by Helen Swansbourne
Production by Bonnie Murray

Printed by 1010 Printing International Ltd on
behalf of Compass Press Ltd

Acknowledgements

The content of this book derives mainly from contributions from Old Seniors and others
connected with the school, as well as the school Archives. Much enthusiasm has been
generated, and the quantity and quality of the material we received has made selecting and
editing the entries a huge and difficult task. Wherever possible we have put names to
individual contributions, but in some cases the published version is a composite drawn
together from several accounts: it has been endlessly fascinating to read different versions
of the same event or the same situation. All the contributions will form a valuable addition
to the school Archives.

The staff at Downe House have been extremely helpful, especially Kate Finlay, Dave Fyffe,
Andrea Hudson, and Gordon Roberts. Mary Midgley was kind enough to give us permission
to include extracts from her memoir, *The Owl of Minerva*, published in 2005 by Routledge, to
whom we are also very grateful for permission to use this material. We are grateful also to
Kate Denholm for permission to use part of the score of a piece she composed while at
school. At Third Millennium Information, many thanks are due to David Burt, who has been
a tower of strength in getting the project off the ground in the first place and in keeping it
on track, and to Bonnie Murray, whose high production standards have ensured a splendid
final product. Finally, we were entranced by Helen Swansbourne's sensitive and beautiful
design, and are hugely grateful for her expertise and help.

Picture acknowledgements

All photographs and other illustrated material are copyright © Downe House School, with
the exception of the school photograph of 2005 (pages 168–9) © Gillman & Soame, and the
many images throughout the book taken by Gordon Roberts who has kindly given
permission for their use. His work – along with that of David Fyffe – on the restoration of
the archive material is also much appreciated.

Many of the illustrations were supplied by the school Archives, which have been consid-
erably enhanced by the images provided by the following: Juliet Austin, Alison Bartholomew,
Jean Brandon, Pearl Brewin, Valerie Byrom-Taylor, Susan Cameron, Olivia Clifton-Bligh,
Mike Delacole, Elizabeth Dickson, Huw Evans, Gillian Feary, Sue Foote, Diana Gifford
Mead, Frances Green, Annabel Gray, Elizabeth Gray, Alison Gwatkin, Caroline Horsbrugh,
Rosemary Kimmins, Nicola Lovell, Anna Markwell, Katharine McCulloch, Alicia Meeke,
R Melly, Cherry Palmer, Saranne Piccaver, the Piper family, Judy Powell, Rosemary Powell,
Paul and Clare Risoe, Lucinda Tindley, Penny Trance, Rosemary Tredgold, Judith Wheaton,
Cynthia Wood, Sue Woodroffe. We have used as many of these images as possible in the
book, and all of them have been copied and retained in the Archives.

Every effort has been made to trace and credit copyright holders; we will be pleased to
correct any unintentional errors or omissions in subsequent editions of this book.

Contents

9   CHAPTER 1
Origins, foundation, and the Kent years

27   CHAPTER 2
Downe House at Cold Ash

57   CHAPTER 3
Changing times

93   CHAPTER 4
A new beginning

127   CHAPTER 5
Other perspectives

153 CHAPTER 6
Broadening horizons

166 EPILOGUE

170 GLOSSARY

171 LIST OF SUBSCRIBERS

175 INDEX OF NAMES AND TOPICS

Editors' note

'Yet Olive Willis remains a mystery and a miracle. God with her, with grace and strength she did what she did, was as she was.'

So wrote Elizabeth Bowen in her Foreword to Anne Ridler's *Olive Willis and Downe House*, published in 1967 at the behest of Miss Willis's sister, Dorothy. Forty years on, as Downe House prepares to celebrate its centenary, the vision and ethos of its powerful, remarkable, idiosyncratic founder are still palpable, still part of what makes Downe House unique.

But Downe House is also different now: still true to that original vision but also bearing the stamp of other impressive women (and men) who have carried on developing and moulding it, and driving it forward into the twenty-first century and into the future. 'Olive Willis wanted to create a school where each individual within the community mattered and where relations between staff and pupils should be normal.' Well, so she did, and so it remains. And while it is true that some of her revolutionary ideas no longer operate in quite the way they did during the nearly forty years of her reign as Headmistress, the vision that created them is still there, underpinning and strengthening a thoroughly modern school.

This is not a straightforward history of Downe House; rather it is a celebration, through memories, reminiscences, anecdotes, and insights, of the first century in the life of a unique institution. The history of the school is the backdrop; but it is enhanced and brought to life through the contributions of those who taught and studied there. Requests for material resulted in a deluge, and we have included as much as we can. And, as editors, we have enjoyed the huge benefit of being able to draw both on Anne Ridler's biography of Olive Willis and her school, and on the *Downe House Scrap-Book*, edited by Alison Linklater and published to celebrate the school's first fifty years in 1957. The *Scrap-Book* contains contributions by the very first pupil to join the school in 1907 as well as by other alumnae of the first five decades – and by Miss Willis herself. Here is just one, by Jocelyn Baber (Ashley Dodd, 1920), who came to Downe at the age of nine in 1913 and remained there for eight years: 'One day my particular friend and I had a tremendous fight in the Sand Walk, rolling over and over and even drawing blood. Miss Willis appeared from nowhere and placidly bade us get up. She announced that both of us forthwith should be provided with boxing-gloves. This was done and for the duration of the craze we drew quite an audience.'

This is typical of the many reminiscences of Olive Willis, who was, of course, the overwhelmingly dominant personality of the first half-century of Downe House. But it is sixty years since she ceased to be Headmistress and over forty years since her death. So the second half-century in the life of the school is just as important and just as weighty, and receives its due prominence here. Life generally, and girls' education in particular, have changed fundamentally and immensely during the last fifty years, and Downe House has responded to those changes and those challenges. There is something here for everyone, of whatever age, who has been part of the first hundred years in the life of the school.

My grandmother, Sybil Stewart, was one of the first pupils at Downe House in Kent. I believe I was one of the first grand-daughters at the school when I was there from 1954 to 1959. My daughter Anna Krasinska (Molesworth-St Aubyn, 1988) was there in the 1980s and was possibly the first great-grand-daughter.

I remember the cold, the runs up the drive after morning chapel, the dread of piano lessons because I hadn't practised. Shivering by the swimming pool . . . and the horror of floppy dancing. But gradually I learnt confidence, how to make lasting friends, the ability to do some things really well without being seen to try too hard, and how to have fun. I realise that Downe gave me a strong base. I am now in my sixties, married for forty-one years, chairman of an NHS Trust, and still curious. I hope it will continue to succeed for another hundred years.

Mary Molesworth-St Aubyn (Meiklejohn, 1959)

CHAPTER 1

Origins, foundation, and the Kent years

10

'I hope you will be clever, because you will never be pretty.' Janet Willis's words to her second daughter, born in 1877, typify Victorian attitudes towards women, whose main aim in life was to attract husbands through their beauty and their accomplishments as potential wives and mothers. Cleverness was less desirable: as the first Principal of Lady Margaret Hall, Elizabeth Wordsworth, said to the mother of a prospective student, 'I feel it my duty to tell you, dear Mrs X, that our girls do not marry well.' Education for girls and young women was in its infancy, and although women were increasingly being allowed to study at university, by no means all institutions at the end of the nineteenth century awarded them degrees.

Olive was clever, and also headstrong, and was sent to school at Wimbledon House, later to become Roedean. Much of her experience there was to find later reflection in her own school: she rejected the exaggerated emphasis on games, the house system, the myriad petty rules, the elaborate prefect system, and the lack of any religious dimension to teaching or discussion; but she did follow many of the

Olive Willis in 1881, aged 4

Downe House, Kent, in 1909, painted by Dorothy Willis

The room we used as a Common Room was the famous study, where Charles Darwin wrote *On the Origin of Species*. We still called it the Study, and it was there we pursued our humble activities, read, worked, and corrected. Olive and her staff had dinner there in the evenings and the meals at the round table were very enjoyable.

In the evenings Miss Willis used to read aloud in the Drawing Room while the school mended, and I recall an occasional Sunday evening hymn-singing here also, once at least conducted by Miss Willis in a manner all her own. She announced that she was going to play the accompaniment. This surprised us all: no-one knew that she could play the piano. She called for a suggestion as to a hymn. One was hazarded. Miss Willis found the place, started to play, came to a stop, started again, and finally turned round in a most unconcerned way. 'No, that's much too difficult. Think of another one.'

Winifred Morgan-Brown (Teacher, 1909–20)

12

Olive Willis in 1907

The Drawing Room, Downe House, Kent

Roedean ways, such as the division of lessons into forty-minute periods called 'forties' and weekly free days for all members of staff. And she adopted a Roedean-style uniform, the djibbah, which was to persist at Downe House until the late 1970s.

She went up to Somerville in 1898 to read history where, despite her lack of sporting prowess at Roedean, she became an enthusiastic hockey player. Alice Carver, a fellow player who was also a member, and later captain, of the England hockey team, was to become her first partner at Downe House. After graduating, Olive taught in a variety of schools, including Queen Anne's and Roedean, and – anxious to gain experience of a different kind – in state schools in London as a supply teacher. She was already harbouring the notion of opening her own school, and her principles were becoming established: at both boarding schools she was criticised for fostering real friendships between staff and pupils and for seeking to stimulate and interest the girls in subjects outside the school curriculum. As one of her later pupils at

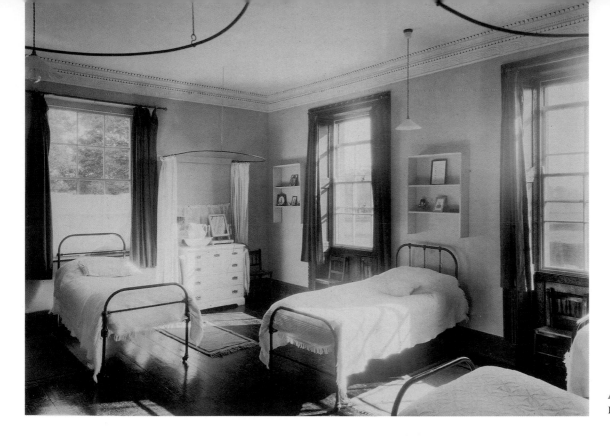

A bedroom at Downe
House, Kent

Downe, Priscilla Napier (Hayter, 1926), recorded in the *Scrap-Book*, 'I had been well taught before Downe, but the lessons of Miss Willis were a revelation to me of what teaching could be. It was as if one had swum suddenly out of a narrow river into the limitless sea.'

By 1906, Olive Willis and Alice Carver were ready to take the plunge of setting up their own school. Their fathers both agreed to advance £1,500 each, and in due course a suitable building was found: Downe House in north Kent, Charles Darwin's former home. It was ideal: in the country but within easy reach of London; big enough for their planned thirty or so pupils; surrounded by its own twenty-two acres of ground; and with close associations to a great scientist whose seminal work, *On the Origin of Species*, had been written there. The deal was done in February 1907, and Miss Willis and Miss Carver set about issuing a prospectus and recruiting staff.

They soon had staff in place, though some of them were at this stage part-time. Miss Heather taught science and mathematics, Miss Lane was the games mistress, Miss Collins taught English literature and some music, and Miss Willis taught French, Latin, scripture, and history as well as some English. Miss Carver acted as matron and managed the household affairs, and augmented the strength of physical education at the school. Indeed, the first Inspectors' Report commented on the high standard the school had already attained in physical education. It was not to be long before

The Dining Room at
Downe House, Kent

Alice Carver

Lilian Heather

14

To a lanky lamp-post of a girl in that strange garment, a djibbah, school with no other girls might well have been an ordeal, but nothing could have been further from the case. We were a very happy family and I have a shrewd suspicion that I was more than a little spoilt; the staff – five residents and more visiting – were young and gay and the days were full of fun and exciting things to do. I was an outdoor child accustomed to running wild and I dreaded the restrictions of school but there were none, and this sense of freedom is still, to my mind, one of Downe's greatest attributes – freedom to develop individually but encouraged unconsciously in the right direction.

There are memories of so many things . . . new classrooms were equipped, the playing-field was made, the laboratory in the garden was opened, and here Miss Heather presided over the bangs and smells. What a gifted teacher she was, making even test-tubes and litmus paper interesting, and what an honour to be working in Darwin's own laboratory . . . and how we enjoyed stabling Miss Heather's pony and harnessing him up for her in the evenings.

There were jaunts to the theatre, travelling in a double-decker bus with lively competition for the front seats on top; those drives are a saga in themselves. The country roads seemed to go to the London drivers' heads and the bus would take the bit between its teeth and career down the hills and round the corners. Coming home on snowy roads was an exciting adventure; on one foggy occasion we took it in turn to walk in front of the bus waving a handkerchief to guide the driver.

Nan Napier (Woodall, 1910)

Downe House was to play and beat Roedean's second cricket XI.

The first pupil was Nan Napier (Woodall, 1910; seen in the 1909 school photograph on page 168, third from the right, behind the staff row), who was joined for a term by Dulcie Travers and Hilary Willis, a cousin of Olive's, and soon after by Alice Moore, together with her mother and her younger brother, who helped to populate the empty rooms and make the place feel lived in. Others followed, and by the end of two years the school had reached the planned number of thirty. By 1914 there were forty-two pupils and by 1918 fifty-two. Fees were fifty guineas a term, the norm for the time.

The partnership with Alice Carver was not ideal: the two women complemented each other but also clashed, and Miss Carver's delicate health began to suffer under the strain; she left in 1912. The second-in-command role was filled first by Winifred Morgan-Brown and then by Lilian Heather, who was – as Olive Willis wrote in the *Scrap-Book* – 'then and always the best teacher in the school'. She taught science in Darwin's laboratory, and treated all her pupils, regardless of their prowess in her subject, with care and solicitude. 'Now someone has made a very interesting mistake . . .' must be the best and kindest approach any teacher might make to a floundering pupil.

And then came Miss Nickel. Originally engaged in 1912 to teach geography, she was, as Miss Willis says, '. . . always a mysterious figure. No-one will ever know where she came from and she herself had obviously taken a vow of silence about the past. I realised before long that she was very little use as a teacher, but she was a skilled craftsman and could inspire people in every practical way.' She became the school's handyman and builder, both in Kent and later at Cold Ash.

The traditions of Downe House were firmly laid down during those early years: readings by Miss Willis round the Drawing Room fire while the girls sewed and mended their clothes, augmented on a Sunday by coffee brewed in a Turkish

Miss Nickel

Certainly the oddest member of Downe House staff to join in the first years of the school's existence was Maria Nickel, recruited initially as a geography teacher but soon to become architect, chauffeur, and handyman. She was a mysterious figure: no one ever used her first name and no one knew where she came from, beyond the fact that she had probably been born in Poland and mostly been brought up in Russia. She was, however, a highly educated woman – she spoke twenty-three languages – and a skilled craftswoman, and soon began both to put up new buildings and to maintain the school's fabric. As Miss Willis says, somewhat drily, in the *Scrap-Book*, 'In everything she did there was a touch of genius and equally an inability to complete a bit of work. . . . There was always an original touch in Miss Nickel's work and in her methods.'

She was never seen with her head uncovered; her grey felt hats were made for her by Scotts of Piccadilly. Her invariable dress was a brownish serge overall, belted and reaching nearly to her ankles, usually stained with oil and with a packet of cigarettes tucked into the breast pocket. As Mary Midgley (Scrutton, 1937) recalls in her memoir, *The Owl of Minerva*, 'In my time she looked more like a sinister priest in a Goya etching. . . . Her habit of constantly muttering to herself enhanced the priestly or magical effect she made as, with a cigarette in the corner of her mouth, she prowled endlessly around the place on her lawful occasions.'

Her driving was hair-raising: as Miss Willis recalls, 'she had never become used to driving on the left-hand side of the road.' And she was occasionally inclined to exploit the position of power her status as the chauffeur gave her: arrivals of whom she did not approve were sometimes left to walk the five miles from the nearest station.

Legend had it that she slept on the mat outside Miss Willis's bathroom, as a guardian. It seems that in truth she did sleep on the bathroom floor, because she believed that sleeping on wood was good for her rheumatism. Later, to avoid draughts, she placed a sheet of wood on top of the bath and slept there. After the school's move to Berkshire she slept in the hall like a watchdog, and was until the end of her life (she died in 1946) a guardian presence in the hallway of Miss Willis's own house.

She was devoted to Miss Willis and to the school. Everyone always rushed round at the beginning of a term to see what new addition she had contrived, and, at the new Downe House, she was wont to appear out of the well-house in the middle of the drive like a jack-in-the-box as cars drove up to the door. Her buildings were solid and often proved hard to demolish when they had to be changed or extended; Miss Farr recalls that the builders employed to remodel one of her buildings when Tedworth was being constructed came back twice with revised estimates because they found the demolition work so difficult. Many of the possibly somewhat eccentric twists and turns evident to this day in Downe's architecture are the result of Miss Nickel's ingenuity in dealing with the difficulties of the terrain.

Her softer side is fondly remembered. She was an excellent cook, and taught her pupils to make light puff pastry and delicious steak and kidney puddings stuffed with cloves. As Jocelyn Baber (Ashley-Dodd, 1920) recalls, 'I don't think many people know, though I had experience of this, that she could be both doctor and nurse, of infinite gentleness and very deft.' And another scared new pupil, fresh from Brazil, was much comforted when Miss Nickel swept her up, talked to her in her own language, and introduced her to the school.

Dogs and other pets

Miss Willis and three of her Samoyeds

Dogs were an inseparable part of Downe House for most of the first hundred years. When the school opened Miss Willis had an 'unruly terrier, misnamed Seraphina' (according to Anne Ridler) whose constant, devoted companion was Tiger, the bull mastiff belonging to Nan Napier (Woodall, 1910) which she had been allowed to bring to school. The two ranged the countryside together, and 'Pheena' later sadly died while giving birth to Tiger's puppies.

Miss Willis later had large white Samoyeds, whose care was in the hands of Miss Nickel. Memories of her calling the dogs – who seem to have been very disobedient – are legion among pupils of the 1930s and the war years. Delle Fletcher (Chenevix-Trench, 1933) recalls taking the dogs with them on walks, but that as no one had ever inculcated obedience in them, they would invariably return with one missing – usually Boris. Neither Miss Nickel nor Miss Heather had much luck with Boris, and his name was frequently to be heard echoing through the local woodland as they searched for him. Jill Lewis (Bradfield, 1935) remembers the 'dog palace' the Samoyeds lived in near the main buildings. It was a large, wired-in enclosure with a two-storey, chalet-style house with a roof and staircase but no outside walls.

Janet Ellen (Pearson, 1935) writes: 'In 1932 my form was given permission to keep pets. The reason, we vaguely understood, was because we were difficult to deal with at times, supposedly because we were 'war babies' whose home life had suffered from our fathers being away for long periods fighting the war. We were delighted, and the pets varied from budgerigars to a bushbaby. My friend Elizabeth and I decided to share a rabbit. Benjamin was a plump, grey, gentle rabbit. One day, when Elizabeth was isolated in her bedroom with an infection, she pushed an SOS under my bedroom door. 'Something AWFUL has happened to Benjy – the white dogs were barking round his hutch this morning. Do go and see if he is all right.' I found a very different Benjy – grey, yes, but thin and bouncy, quite unlike our cosy rabbit. We decided to ask Miss Willis if she knew what had happened. She looked at us very sadly: 'Oh! My darling children! I thought you wouldn't notice!'

Later, in the 1940s, although pets were not formally allowed, some girls seem to have been able to bring their dogs to school anyway. Elizabeth Houssemayne du Boulay (Home, 1940) was allowed to have her black and tan terrier, Scamp, at school at the outbreak of war, and she trained him to retrieve cricket balls during matches of the 'also ran' teams. Three

sisters among the Queen's Gate girls also brought their black poodle with them, to the fury of the Samoyeds who invariably attacked him. The poodle did not last long, however, after he bit the Matron and was expelled back to the parental home. Jenny Gosse also managed to flout the rules: 'It was in my second term and I knew very well that pets were not allowed, but I managed to smuggle my white mice into my bedroom where they were rapidly discovered. Sent to explain myself to Miss Willis, I found a stern but not unsympathetic hearing and it was then that Alfred Gadd, the school carpenter, made a superb, two-roomed mouse-palace for the undeserving, at Miss Willis's bidding.'

The resident staff continued to keep dogs. Miss Gunn's little dog, Trot, was in constant attendance at lessons – 'a dog is a great help in teaching', as she would frequently say – and would bark approval at the end of a piece, or once, as a pupil recalls, 'to its great embarrassment, at the halfway double bar'. Mrs Wilson had a spaniel and Miss Farr had several dogs, notably Irish Setters. Miss Cameron's Springer Spaniels sprawled out in the sunshine were an immediate attraction to one prospective pupil and her father, and resident staff kept dogs with them in their Houses if they wished to.

Gardening in Kent

Removes with Miss Farr's dogs in the 1980s

pot; Miss Willis herself tucking up and kissing goodnight every single child; prolonged hair brushing before bedtime; individual 'jaws' at the end of each term; walks punctuated by vain cries for unheeding dogs to come to heel . . .

Olive Willis disliked the excesses of competition, so Downe awarded no prizes. There was, however, a system of stars and stripes for good work and bad behaviour, marked weekly for each form on a sort of balance sheet. If stars outweighed stripes, the whole form had a day's holiday; if there were too many stripes the individuals responsible were mildly punished, usually by outdoor work in the garden or on the buildings on Saturday afternoon. 'There were many singular stripes given in my time,' Jocelyn Baber (Ashley Dodd, 1920) recalls, 'one of which was for eating an apple without galoshes. It meant, of course, that someone had gone out in break, in the wet, improperly shod.'

Hockey in Kent

Miss Willis also disliked the rigid prefect system which was then the norm in both boys' and girls' schools. But three years after the school opened she introduced her system of self-government, whereby a small number of 'Seniors' were to be elected from the Sixth Form by the whole school. The Seniors were responsible for a certain amount of administration and discipline, though without the right to inflict punishment, and there was never, in those early days, a Head Girl; the eldest acted as spokesman for the other Seniors when the need arose. Moreover, all girls who had been at the school for more than a year were to be given the title of Old Senior when they left.

This enlightened system worked well and persists, in essence, to the present day. The votes, until recently, were weighted and sometimes adjusted, but mainly in order to give someone who might narrowly have missed it the chance of responsibility. As Priscilla Napier (Hayter, 1926) notes in the *Scrap-Book*, 'Miss Willis was supplied with a sort of Gallup Poll of the state of opinion in the school, and the school had the illusion of self-government without the burden of having to live under its grosser mistakes.'

Miss Willis sought to keep the horrors and rigours of the First World War away from her pupils, while also wishing them to take its issues seriously. It was not, in truth, far away. On still summer nights the dull boom of the barrage in

Miss Nickel, a wonderful person, ran up buildings as other people ran up dresses. I always wondered what nationality she was – I thought maybe Tartar with Polish, as she was rather yellow.

Miss Willis did not like rules. Her attitude was, 'My darling child, you cannot be stupid enough to require rules.' She also had a wonderful sense of humour. We did one play which had a secret society in it which needed a secret sign so that the members would recognise one another. Miss Willis suggested that members should lie on their backs with their legs in the air. [Eds: In the 1980s the girls still did this, usually in the Dining Room; they called it Dead Ants.]

On Miss Willis's birthday there was a short-lived tradition that a play was performed in which every girl in the school had a speaking part. This got more difficult as the school got larger. In 1916 the problem was solved by having a musical with three heroines and three heroes who appeared together in a row throughout. One year we did *Alcestis* on the Mound in the garden which had trees growing on it. It was produced by Miss Morgan-Brown who made the Greek costumes for the whole cast.

We played lacrosse and hockey in the winter and tennis and cricket in the summer. I wasn't very good, but at a Fathers' cricket match I ran my father out.

Sibella Bonham-Carter, 1916
[Extracts from an interview in 2003 when she was 103]

Jaws

There are vivid memories of 'jaws', the termly individual interviews with Miss Willis which everyone had to undergo. Some memories are imbued with gratitude and pleasure, others with horror; they were occasions for trembling and fear, but also for uplifting, confidence-boosting discussions. Jocelyn Baber (Ashley Dodd, 1920) recalls: 'At the end of each term, everyone had to knock when they reached the top of the queue for the "jaws". When we were young and turbulent or when older and "not contributing to the life of the school" or in some other way unsatisfactory, we squirmed and writhed with shame or indignation. But to some, particularly when they had reached the stage of discussing a career, the "jaw" was a joy, a support, and an inspiration. I suppose it was then that Miss Willis trained her phenomenal memory which allowed her later to welcome several hundred of us, in any order and of any age, with complete intimacy and knowledge.'

Catherine Sandford (Hunt, 1941) was less impressed: 'Olive Willis clearly thought me unexceptionally ordinary and said I should become a theologian. I fear I had more worldly ideas and became a Wren.' Diana Peper (Selby, 1949) was one who experienced Miss Willis's final admonishments: 'During her last jaw before retirement girls were stumbling weeping out of her study because they were so moved by her final advice. When it came to me she stared for a long time out of the window, braced her shoulders, and said, "Diana, can't you try even for one moment to look less vacant?" That remark stayed with me, and my subsequent school career was not exactly glorious! But Miss Medley later rescued my self-esteem when, after I had made the position of Senior by the school's vote, she decided to uphold the vote in order to put "the good of Diana" before what she might have decided was "the good of the school". I was so proud, and so happy during my last two terms at Downe.'

Miss Medley continued the 'jaws' for at least part of her tenure, but they were discontinued during Mrs Wilson's time, evolving instead into school assembly at the beginning and end of each term which became known as the School Jaw. Miss Farr disliked the term and discouraged its use, despite the attempts of some traditionalists to return to 'djibbahs and jaws'.

Nancy Medley

Flanders could be heard, and noise from the new aerodrome at Biggin Hill became another distraction. One afternoon it came even closer, when an aircraft circled low over the girls playing hockey and dropped a message: 'Dear Hockey Girls, ask your headmistress if you may come to the aerodrome, we would like to show you around.' Most headmistresses at that time would have said an immediate 'no' to such an invitation, but Miss Willis readily agreed to let the girls go, and there followed several trips to the aerodrome. They also witnessed a Zeppelin brought down in flames by aircraft from Biggin Hill.

Olive Willis always preferred the personal touch. She spent a lot of time interviewing potential new parents, and many of them became her friends. And apart from tucking up all her children in bed at night, she instituted the termly 'jaws' – private, individual interviews in which she sought to encourage, mould, and influence her

Detail of the school photograph in 1920; the staff sitting in the middle row include, from left, Madame, Miss Havergal, Miss Morgan-Brown, Miss Moore, Miss Read, Miss Gunn, Miss Heather, Miss Willis, Miss Croft, and Miss Oliver; the others cannot currently be identified

20

I suppose I had from the beginning a sort of dread of anything which could feel like 'an institution' – therefore I feel it a tribute to Miss Nickel to say that her outbuildings had a Kafka-like oddness. Their acoustics, their perspectives, their ventilation were peculiar to themselves. Not less, there was something in an elegant way ramshackle about the main Downe House . . . and one reason why the move from the old Downe to the present Downe was made was that we girls were beginning to wear out the fabric of the house. There cannot have been many more than seventy of us, but even so our cattle-like gatherings and stampedings were sufficient to make the structure rock. 'Need you *rush*?' Miss Willis constantly used to say, looking at us with a distaste which concealed affection.

Miss Willis's attitude, throughout, was far less 'Don't' than 'Need you?' There was always something speculative, detached, about her criticisms, which was probably why they took such deep effect with us. In fact, they were not so much criticisms as invitations – to be taken up or not as we thought well – to criticise ourselves, plus suggestions (only just not tentative) as to what lines to take if we chose to do so.

Elizabeth Bowen, 1917

pupils. She abhorred complacency and self-satisfaction: in a letter to a girl of whom she was very fond she wrote: 'It is just that self-complacency that I have always wanted to see you break down (I admit I have hurled a good many things at it, in the hope of helping you in the job).'

This personal touch was fundamental to Olive Willis's philosophy; she fostered a family atmosphere as long as she could, but as the school

Gaily, confidently, I approached Miss Willis's door, only hoping that I would find her within and disengaged. I was given a welcome which warms me to recall, to this day. 'For our Forsaken Merman', I said, 'I am doing a dance. Might I borrow your green scarf?' 'Yes of course. What else are you going to wear?' 'Well we thought – it's under the sea, with green net between us and the audience – just my hair.' It was true that my hair was then very long and thick, but as Miss Willis explained that some fathers might be present, she suggested that I add something to the scarf.

Jocelyn Baber (Ashley Dodd, 1920)

became larger this ideal was more difficult to achieve. There was, however, a new young teacher who joined the school halfway through the war whose special gift, during the nearly fifty years she was there, was to provide a taste of home to the young and nervous. This was Winona Croft, at first known as 'Caw' and later as 'Crift', who taught geography and maths to the lower forms, and later weaving, and was also a musician. She

Olive Willis and one of her letters

became a mainstay of the school's welfare, fondly remembered by generations of shy, scared, homesick newcomers whom she took under her wing and cherished.

The school was getting into its stride. But it was also beginning to burst at the seams, and the noise from Biggin Hill was increasing. It became clear that a new home would have to be found.

Uniform

The djibbah, copied from Roedean, was the main part of the Downe House uniform from the beginning until the late 1970s. Made by Sheba of Sloane Street, it was a thick woollen garment with a yoke embroidered with the Downe House shield, and it fell from the shoulder over the bust, with no belt. 'They were not pretty, but we were very fond of them,' is a constant recollection, as is the observation that they were very practical for teenage girls of all shapes and sizes. The point was to have an old djibbah: as Jennifer Hollings (Hutt, 1947) writes, 'It was a matter of prestige to have an old and multi-patched djibbah, and I was miserable when my unsympathetic mother wasted clothing coupons on getting me a new one which was not nearly as smart to the discriminating eye.' They started with deep hems which were let down as their owners grew, and they were patched again and again as the wool, particularly at the back of the skirt, wore out on hard school chairs. It was not unknown for coach drivers to remark on the scruffy appearance of the girls from what they thought was an expensive school! This

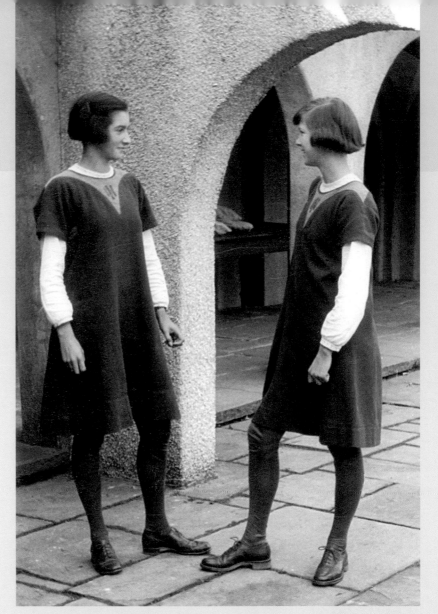

Djibbahs in the 1930s, above, and modelled by today's girls, left

From

Sloane 3132

173, Sloane Street
S.W.1.

SHEBA

M⁰. J. Mc Swiny

Four Winds

Roxborough Path

Harrow, Middx

scruffiness was not helped by the custom of storing all the term's letters in the djibbah pocket, which became floppy and distorted as a result.

Miss Willis said of the djibbah that she tried to alter the design so that it would be less difficult to make, but her efforts fell on stony ground. 'Do not blame me if you find djibbahs distasteful,' she wrote in the *Scrap-Book*. Her first pupil longed for a complete school uniform, so purple blanket coats, made in Northern Ireland, were commissioned, together with purple felt hats. It is often thought that the school colours, purple and green, were chosen in support of the Suffragettes, but Miss Willis herself said this was not the case: the colours represented Scottish heather, to celebrate her own and Miss Carver's pride in their Scottish ancestry.

Sheba also made the summer uniform, which evolved into cotton tunics of a standard design but in any colour their wearers wished. Summer school photographs were, as a result, a riot of colour. Brown leather belts, *de rigueur* with the summer uniform in the 1940s and 1950s on formal occasions, had to be worn at just the right height from the ground during displays so that all the belts were at the same level.

Long- and short-sleeved white blouses were worn under djibbahs and tunics, embroidered around the neck in green and purple, and without collars or cuffs (to help with ironing). Then there were the essential thick woollen cloaks in winter, green lined with red, which replaced the purple coats during the Second World War. The cloaks were by tradition never buttoned up when worn over the shoulders, but were buttoned round the waist when they were worn in class as long skirts, to keep out the cold. Frances Dowson (Green, 1959) recalls that 'cloaks which had differently coloured linings seemed the height of sophistication; the few that sported tartan linings were truly exotic.' She also records: 'The Head Senior "inherited" the purple jersey to go over her djibbah. This was threadbare and darned, but much the most important part of the jersey was the assortment of name-tapes of past Head Seniors culminating in the incumbent's. Rumour had it that the jersey would disintegrate if it was washed.' This historic jersey survived until the mid-1990s when, sadly, it disappeared.

Trunks were sent ahead PLA – Passenger Luggage in Advance – and there were rituals involved in unpacking them the day after arrival. Gill Grimes (Townend, 1948) remembers unpacking in Ancren Gate the day after she arrived at Downe at the age of nine. 'Each of us with our school trunks had to lay our clothes in piles on our bed to be checked for name-tapes and numbers. Three pairs of most things including three pairs of white knicker linings and three pairs of green knickers to go on top.' Her sister Elizabeth Knowler (Townend, 1943) remembers that 'blue legs were almost as much a part of Downe as the djibbah, as it was the "in" thing

23

Packing and laundry lists, 1957

to wear only ankle socks at all times, regardless of the weather.'

Celia Edey (Green, 1963) writes poetically about the djibbah: 'It is my first morning at Downe and the first time I am to wear my djibbah. I remember the dusty corner of London where a few months ago I was measured, and I know that this one has been woven and made for me and me alone. I put on my collarless, cuffless, long-sleeved blouse with the green and purple embroidery round neck and wrists and pull my green djibbah over my head. It feels stiff and slightly scratchy, the hem comes well down my calves, the large patch-pocket lies flat on my right-hand thigh. The "DHS" embroidered in purple on my chest proclaims proudly that I am now well and truly "at Downe". Six years later – same djibbah. Now the back is criss-crossed with machine stitching and there is a large patch on the inside – meticulously executed by Hattie in the Gallery with her foot-pedal sewing machine, her way of prolonging the life of a djibbah whose seat has worn too thin. Now the hem is above my knees and the pocket at my waist gapes open – that vital pocket which has housed every letter I receive each term. Except for Hattie's handiwork, the material is soft and pliant, the green slightly faded, but now I know that the choice of purple on green for the "DHS" reflects the colours of the suffragette movement [but see above – Eds] – and I wear it with a different pride. I connect to the independent women who pushed the boundaries for us all, and as I take off my djibbah for the last time with nostalgia and sadness, I go forward into the rest of my life with the confidence of all Old Seniors, past and future.'

It seems that the end of the djibbah was being rumoured as early as 1957, the fiftieth anniversary of Downe House. The *Magazine* for that year included a Jubilee paean in praise of the djibbah by Margaret Lister (Pryor, 1923): 'I have heard it rumoured the djibbah may be superseded. By what? This is important as nothing could replace it. . . . That great leveller which makes the full blown rose quite as unseen as the blushing violet and doesn't give the orchid any chance. The medley of figures that move across the school scene move without pride of shape, lost in the uniformity of the djibbah, that ingenious garment sans hooks, poppers, buttons, or zips. This is our Jubilee. Downe has been for fifty years, and so has the djibbah. We have no other. We need no other. There must be no other.' Well, it did indeed persist for over twenty years more.

Detail of the school photograph in 1977 with the multicoloured summer tunics

Today's uniform

'By 1957,' writes Gillian Hulbert (Savory, 1962) 'we were customising the djibbah with djibbah jerseys of our own choice and colour, and the lisle stockings had given way to the newly fashionable, gaily coloured tights in any colour. In cold winters fur boots were often added to the ensemble and a cheerful coloured duffle coat. We looked dreadful! In summer Sheba provided linen tunics of any colour worn with a leather belt and short-sleeved djibbah blouses of floppy cotton. These were largely unworn, as Sister decreed when you could wear summer uniform and it never seemed to be before the end of May.'

By the late 1970s djibbahs had become not only extremely expensive but outmoded and impractical. With the arrival of Miss Farr, a new uniform was introduced, with the school colours changing from green and purple to green and red. The everyday uniform was a dark green skirt, a green-and-white striped shirt, and either a green or a red V-necked sweater. This uniform is broadly the same now, although the skirt is now a kilt. The green cloaks with red linings continued until the early 1990s. The green blazers with a red stripe, introduced with these initial changes, are still worn.

Summer uniform has also changed and is now the same as that worn in winter, apart from short-sleeved shirts. Miss Farr introduced a new Sixth Form uniform consisting of a kilt in any colour worn with a shirt with a collar and a toning V-necked sweater. They now wear long black skirts and a black jacket.

Miss Farr also introduced gowns for the Seniors. These were dark green and have become part of the school's heritage in that succeeding owners add their name-tapes to those of their predecessors. Since then, dark blue gowns have been introduced for the Chapel Seniors and, most recently, dark red gowns for the School Ambassadors.

Sixth Form kilts in 1990

Sixth Formers in 2006 wearing their official gowns: green for Seniors, blue for Chapel Seniors, and red for Ambassadors

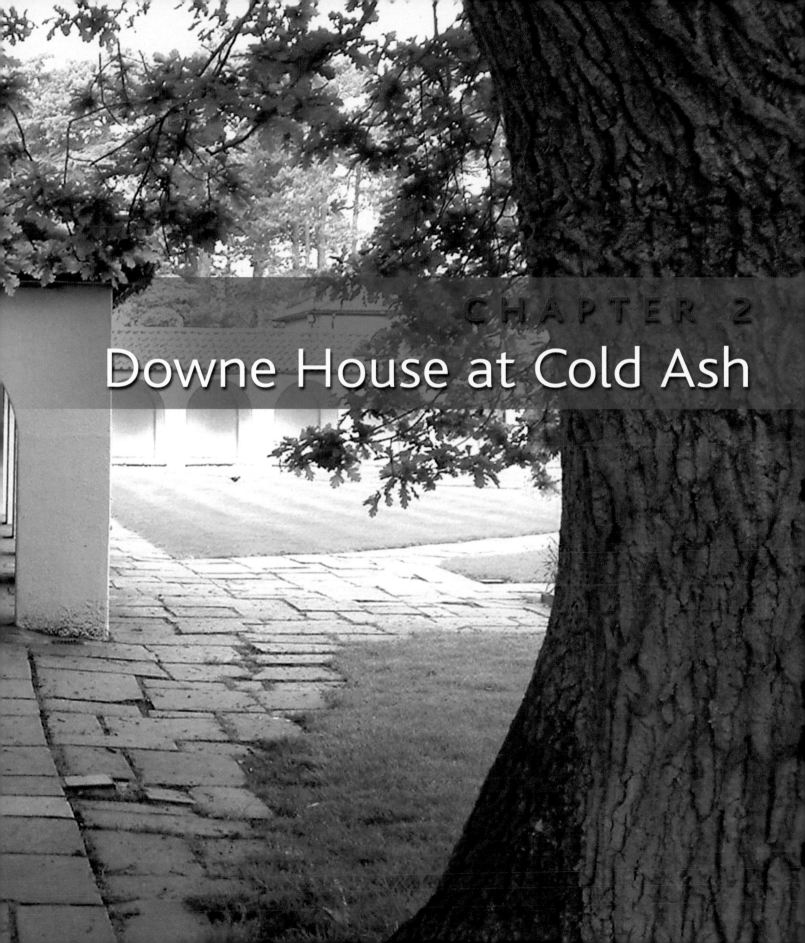

CHAPTER 2

Downe House at Cold Ash

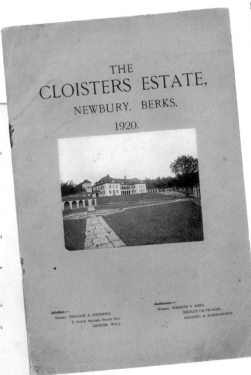

28

live Willis wanted the new school to be on a hill, in real country, and yet within reach of a town and a railway station. In 1921 her sister Dorothy, while spending time with a friend in Berkshire, came across a house for sale that met all these requirements, and moreover was in a glorious position with tremendous views.

This was 'The Cloisters', which stood – and stands – on a fir-topped hill at Cold Ash, near Newbury. It had been built during the First World War for an organisation which called itself the 'School of Silence' but had fallen victim to financial troubles. The roughcast surfaces of the buildings and the red Mediterranean-style roof tiles,

which had suited the monastic aspirations of the order, were attractive, and the Cloisters themselves were to become an admirable setting for plays and gymnastic displays. To add to its attractions, the less than monastic interior, with its thirty-six well-equipped bedrooms and twelve bathrooms, was ideal for the school – if initially far too small.

After some haggling and delay, the purchase was completed in December 1921 and Miss Nickel immediately moved in and started to alter and build. Many of her additions to the property in Kent – including the Chapel – were dismantled and transported to the new school, and the move was accomplished during the Easter holidays of 1922. Water was an initial problem during that first dry summer, until Miss Nickel drove a deep borehole close to the original water tower and struck an excellent source. And there was not yet enough accommodation for everyone: many of the new residents, both staff and pupils, had no option other than to sleep outside during that first term.

But buildings soon went up, and teaching and living accommodation was occupied. Above all, the new school offered endless possibilities for the girls to enjoy the surrounding countryside: the grounds themselves consisted of over 100 acres of woodland and open hillside, and the far-spreading woods beyond the school were also theirs to explore. It was now that the pupils began to experience the freedom for which Downe House at this time and later is so often extolled. So long as they did not go beyond the Bath road and were in groups of at least three – one to stay with anyone who was hurt and the third to run for help – they

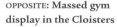

NEAR NEWBURY, BERKS.
On the heights of Cold Ash, 520 feet above sea level. About 4½ miles from Newbury and 16 from Reading.

Illustrated Particulars, Plan & Conditions of Sale
OF

The Cloisters Estate,

comprising altogether a total area of about

235 Acres,

occupying a most commanding position with magnificent views of great expanse and beauty, and including the Residence, known as

"The Cloisters"

Entrance Lodge and beautifully timbered grounds, with a compact private Residence known as

"THE WARDEN'S LODGE,"

COLD ASH FARM,

with excellent Homestead and Farmery, Two other Residences, known as

ST. PETER'S and ANCREN GATE,

all with complete Water Supply, and, as regards The Cloisters and Warden's Lodge, Electric Light and Central Heating, also

A Valuable Building Site.

For Sale by Auction by

MESSRS. SIMMONS & SONS,

AT THE QUEEN'S HOTEL, NEWBURY,
On THURSDAY, OCTOBER 14th, 1920, at 3 o'clock.
(unless previously sold privately).

Solicitors: Auctioneers:
Messrs. PEACOCK & GODDARD,   Messrs. SIMMONS & SONS,
5, South Square, Grays Inn,   Henley-on-Thames,
London, W.C.1.   Reading and Basingstoke.

THE
CLOISTERS ESTATE,
NEWBURY, BERKS.
1920.

Solicitors:—   Auctioneers:—
Messrs. PEACOCK & GODDARD,   Messrs. SIMMONS & SONS,
5, South Square, Grays Inn,   HENLEY-ON-THAMES,
LONDON, W.C.1.   READING & BASINGSTOKE.

**School buildings
in 1922**

were free to go more or less where they wished. Often in the summer groups of girls would take their breakfast sausages and cycle off to cook them somewhere in the hills; and anyone who brought a camp bed could sleep out of doors, with the Cloisters handily nearby to shelter in if it rained. Sleeping out under the stars is one of the many happy memories of this period. Alicia Russell (Eustace, 1934) remembers that Elsie, the school gardener, always knew if it would rain, and Mary Midgley (Scrutton, 1937) writes memorably about the stars: 'On winter nights one had only to go outside and there they were – a tremendous light show, twinkling and various, unimaginably far away yet reliably always there. I never got told much about them and I only knew the names of

RIGHT AND OPPOSITE:
**Girls relaxing at the
back of SPQR and on
the Loggia**

the most obvious constellations. But the sense of distance that they gave – the realisation that one was only a tiny part of a vast and beautiful universe – was immensely welcome and reassuring.'

That first summer the school settled into its new home and resumed the activities and the societies that are so essential for a girls' boarding school. Some of the younger children, seeing that the pool in the centre of the Cloisters had water even if their baths did not, sent to Harrods for 'three goldfish, all of different sexes, habituated to an outdoor life'. There were eighty-three pupils that term; and within three years – by the time the school was first inspected at its new location – there were 118.

The inspection noted – somewhat critically – that there was a great deal of time given to games and gymnastics: four periods of gym and one of dancing a week were regarded as a little excessive,

The first memory that is at all vivid when I was a new girl was of the intense cold at Ancren Gate, and going to bed in my bedroom slippers and hoping Miss Croft wouldn't spot their absence under the bed when she came to put out the lights. I remember the music-making and how enraptured I was when the choral society ended their carols with *In Dulce Jubilo* sung in parts as they walked farther away into the dark night until there was silence. I'll never forget the road to Ancren Gate frozen stiff with a white frost rimming all the russet broken bracken; or a huge full moon behind the pines as you listened to Miss Nickel's voice calling to a recalcitrant dog.

Memories of Miss Willis: of her teaching, one theme stands out . . . she encouraged us to try to equip ourselves to render service in some shape or form, to whatever community we afterwards found ourselves in. We were given a purpose in life. We were told why we were put into the world. Our least talent was fostered. And not least, we were shown beauty in art, literature, and music . . . and above all, I can remember her smile.

Betty Crawford (Studholme, 1926)

Chapel

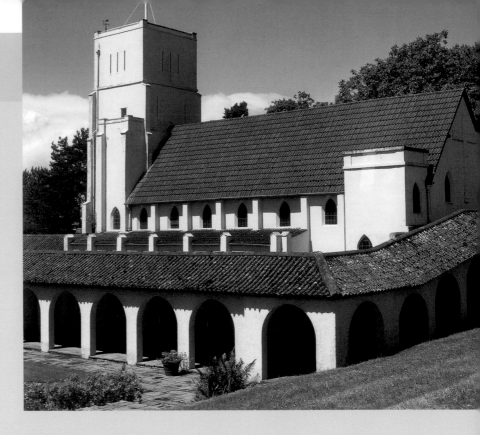

Soon after the school was founded Olive Willis decided that its own Chapel was a priority as soon as the means could be found. From the beginning she used a room at the top of the house for daily school prayers, and she herself preached a sermon on Sundays. One of her staff, who was at first an agnostic, wrote, 'No-one, I think, could have failed to appreciate Miss Willis's reading in Chapel, or her sermons at their best. Her sense of poetry and drama, too, enriched the services. The Chapel was clearly made the centre of the school's life and education.'

Miss Willis made Christianity exciting for her pupils. She was able to do this because she took none of it for granted, but had found and tested it for herself. She once said, 'I have not found anything better than Christianity; if I do, I shall certainly change my religion.' It was this approach that stimulated her pupils. 'I tried to lead girls on to find their own spiritual way. I think that of all studies religion is the most important and the most difficult for any teacher. Instruction must be given but never too dogmatically, and as far as possible by the Socratic method.'

Eleanor Macnair (1939) recalls that, 'On Sunday mornings when we entered Chapel, we were each issued with a threepenny bit which we then put back in the collection bag . . . On one occasion, when there had been a power failure, Miss Willis prayed "Lighten our darkness, we beseech thee, O Lord" and the lights came on.' [Eds: The same threepenny bits were used each time, and the girls were later charged for the term's collections on the bill.]

The Chapel in the 1920s, far left, and the orders of service for its initial dedication in 1916 in Kent and its rededication in 2000

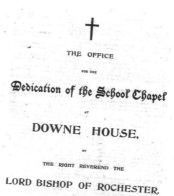

✝

THE OFFICE

FOR THE

Dedication of the School Chapel

AT

DOWNE HOUSE,

BY

THE RIGHT REVEREND THE

LORD BISHOP OF ROCHESTER.

The Feast of the Purification.

Wednesday, February 2nd, 1916.

Downe House

Service of Rededication

by

The Right Reverend Dominic Walker
Bishop of Reading

20th May 2000

Cynthia Wood (Boot, 1942) writes: 'The Chapel was the centre of our life. We had morning and evening prayer, which we all attended. We sang through the Psalms day by day, and I have never forgotten them. On Sundays, Miss Willis took the service and preached. Very seldom, we would have a visiting preacher. The worship was all non-sacramental so, after I was confirmed, we would walk to early service at some local church. I always felt that Downe was a Christian community in action, where you were accepted and could make mistakes, be forgiven, learn, and start again with impunity. I felt very supported and liked, which did me a lot of good.'

Mariella Fischer-Williams (Williams, 1938) has a different take on attitudes to religion at Downe, and the openness which Miss Willis encouraged: 'By the time for confirmation I had doubts about religion. Miss Willis said to me, "Take your bicycle and go to a different church every Sunday and see what you think." I did as I was told. I even took Communion at a Catholic church to see what it would feel like. It felt no different. I was not confirmed. This led my parents to arrange a visit to the Bishop of Oxford; we had nothing to say to each other. My father was a classicist and I think he held no particular belief. The attitude of Olive Willis to my rejection of what she firmly believed in remains for me an outstanding example of openness. I of course continued to take active part in the singing in Chapel and never talked against religion.'

The Chapel has continued to play a fundamental role in the life of the school. The building today would be familiar to all generations, though minor changes have been made. During recent renovations the organ gallery was enlarged and Choral now leads services from on high. A specially commissioned new altar was presented to the school in 2001 and was resited, following modern custom, towards the front of the chancel.

Junior Choral in the Chapel

Dr Fiona Parsons, Sacristan and Head of Religious Studies for twenty years, worked with successive headmistresses and teams of Chapel Seniors to ensure that the girls had every opportunity to develop their knowledge and awareness of religious life. The majority of girls are confirmed during their time at school and gain much from the preparation classes and retreats. Over the years, visiting preachers have provided a tremendous variety of experiences: to listen to a gospel choir one week, followed by a small, voluble, energetic, and venerable (over eighty) nun the next can be most stimulating. Members of staff have played their part, while the Houses have taken their turn in leading regular worship and for many years the Upper Sixth have led memorable and moving Remembrance Day services. In addition, Downe to Earth and other Christian Union groups have been led by girls and staff, and voluntary services, eg weekly Vespers, have been introduced.

For most of its life the school has been greatly helped on a part-time basis by local ministers, especially Philip Allin and John Coombs, who have taken weekly communion services and confirmation classes. In 2004, on Dr Parsons' retirement, a full-time School Chaplain was appointed who quickly became involved with the whole school community. The Chapel remains, as it always has been, a dominant influence.

The new altar dedicated in 2001

Dining Room painting

In her letter introducing the brochure about this book, Clare Balding (1988) talked about 'that funny old place on the hill with the Greek Steps, the Cloisters, and the strange picture at the end of the Dining Room. . .'. That word 'strange' elicited rather pained rejoinders from the daughter and the niece of the artist who painted the pastoral scene – Margaret Lister (Pryor, 1923), who was at Downe both in Kent and at Cold Ash, and later trained at the Slade.

Her niece, Delicia Wallace (Curtis, 1961), records that Margaret was one of five sisters who went to Downe, the eldest of whom, Julia, was one of the first eleven pupils to attend Olive Willis's new school. She adds 'since there were ten in the family altogether, the school has seldom been without a Pryor relative,' a fact attested also by Margaret's daughter, Gulielma Dowrick (Lister, 1961), who writes that she felt that the school was really an extension of her family. 'I had several cousins there, and my late sister also went. I am fascinated that you find the picture strange, but I'm not affronted and nor would my late mother be.'

particularly since games were also played every day except Sunday. Plentiful time was also given to the arts: 'I was allowed to dance and draw to my heart's content,' wrote one girl. 'We were surrounded by music at all times. I associate Downe with pianos and violins echoing from the small music rooms in the Cloisters, the concerts with Myra Hess and Miss Gunn, the wind in the pines . . .'.

Other subjects suffered as a consequence. Not enough time appears to have been given to science and Latin, and timetables made out afresh for each individual each term led to a degree of confusion. 'Look here,' wrote one determined young person (Priscilla Napier (Hayter, 1926)) to her father, 'will you please write seriously to Miss Willis saying *Priscilla must learn Latin*. Because Miss Heather, who is the person who arranges all the lessons, seems determined I shan't learn it.'

Apart from its excellent record in many forms of music, the school maintained consistently high standards in history, the preserve of the charismatic Jean Rowntree, and French, taught at this time by the redoubtable Mlle Agobert, who was tiny, fierce, and terrifying in her elastic-sided boots and the black dress she wore all year round, changing only the collars. 'She smelt abominably, but was very scholarly,' recalls Judith Hubback (Williams, 1934). 'Those of us who spoke French well formed the core of actresses in acts chosen by her from Molière, Corneille, and Racine, which we took to northern French lycées one spring term. She did not think much of Shakespeare who was, she said, barbaric, ie pre-seventeenth century.' Others, including Diana Richmond (Galbraith, 1931), recall 'being terrified by those appalling preps which were slashed by pen-strokes in all directions and finally culminated by the humiliating R for Refaire.'

Crafts were encouraged. Dorothy Willis taught leatherwork and some engraving, as well as running

Sculpting, weaving, and sketching

Shooting

J Holditch Leicester, a retired army colonel who lived near the school, set up a small-bore shooting range in his garden and suggested that some of the girls might like to learn to shoot. Olive Willis, ever open to widening horizons, was delighted with the offer. Colonel Leicester trained the teams to a high standard, to the extent that they won prizes at Bisley. One girl, Mary Darley, was the first girl to win the competition there for those under eighteen.

Colonel Leicester, who later became one of the first members of the Board of Governors in 1944, was a hospitable friend to many of the girls, who called him 'Nunky' (though possibly not to his face) and enjoyed visiting his warm, comfortable home for tea with home-made jam at weekends – particularly in the winter when it made a change from the everlasting cold at the school! Alicia Russell

Colonel 'Nunky' Leicester and Shooting Team

(Eustace, 1934) was one of those whom he taught to shoot and who appreciated his hospitality. She was able to reassure Miss Willis that the colonel was to be trusted: her parents had known him in the Medical Corps in Calcutta.

Colonel Leicester died in 1949, but rifle shooting continued with Reg Piper from Cold Ash Rifle Club which used shooting butts constructed on the local recreation ground. Later, during the 1980s, clay pigeon shooting was introduced, again with great success. One young team – the only all-girls team in the competition – won an award at a national students' competition where they competed with university teams. At the same time, continuing into the 1990s, the CCF cadets shot on both indoor and outdoor ranges.

The shooting team with Reg Piper (on the left) and the safety warden, in the Butts in 1953

Shooting in the prone position, 1939

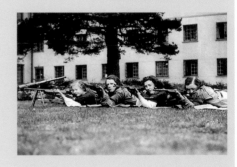

One of Miss Nickel's new buildings under construction

a flourishing sketch club; and weaving too was introduced, regarded by Miss Willis as particularly useful for concentration- and confidence-building, and moreover something at which the less academic girls could excel.

By the autumn of 1923 the gymnasium, a laboratory, and six new classrooms were finished, but it was not until October 1925 that the reconstructed Chapel was ready for dedication. Until that time services took place in the Cloisters, regardless of

> I remember Miss Willis as a progressive headmistress. She trusted us to behave as responsible and reasonable human beings. The school rules always remained implicit – there was never any need to make them explicit or to write them down. This was all part of the ethos of cooperation and living in a community that she engendered. We could develop our talents in this atmosphere of freedom.
>
> I also recall her sense of humour. One evening we organised a quiz for the staff. Miss Heather was there – brilliant at maths, but to look at rather short and plump. One of the questions was, 'What is the pepper pot?' The answer, of course, was the little monument in the garden with the cupola. But Miss Willis replied, 'Oh I know that one – it's Miss Heather, of course.'
>
> **Hester McClintock** (Wilder, 1929)

the weather: Miss Willis was keen on fresh air, though the local vicar who came to officiate was heard to murmur about the primitive conditions – akin, he thought, to the Roman catacombs. Even the Chapel, once built, was not rain-proof for some years – roofs that kept out the rain were never Miss Nickel's strong point, and many are the memories of services accompanied by raindrops tinkling into buckets.

More buildings went up throughout the 1920s and the 1930s; indeed, it was only the onset of war that put a (temporary) end to the building programme. Numbers went up too. Initially to be pegged at 160, there were, by 1939, 250 pupils. The early problems with water and electricity were gradually solved. But Downe House remained cold: as Anne Ridler put it, 'there was still enough cold air to have made an arctic penguin feel at home.' 'Cold' is the word that probably occurs most often in the reminiscences of Old Seniors of this time.

Academic successes were building up too. The school magazine for one year recorded Firsts in Mathematics and Greats at Oxford, and in 1936 a Downe girl passed third into the Civil Service, taking a higher place than any woman had achieved before.

The pepper pot, today and in 1925, and the water tower; watercolours by Dorothy Willis

Early days at Cold Ash: a garden party and swimming

Downe House, lacking the endowments of older foundations, could not offer scholarships to deserving girls who lacked the wherewithal to pay the fees. But there were numbers of pupils who

were taken either free or at reduced rates; only Miss Willis and Miss Heather knew who and how many they were. Joan Gould (Acland, 1940) had the miserable experience, only ten days after arriving at the school in the autumn of 1937, of hearing from Miss Willis that her father had been killed in an aircraft accident. She was then told many years later by her mother that financial considerations should have dictated her leaving Downe then, but that Miss Willis would not hear of it; she kept her on at

I was not one of the world's bright girls, and had I gone to any other school I would have started at the bottom and remained there or been sent away. But Miss Willis was an individualist, who coaxed me into some kind of shape. One time in an English lesson, when she had corrected an appallingly spelled essay of mine, she said 'What a pity you didn't live in Chaucer's day – you have such perfect Chaucerian spelling!' Somehow I reached the top of the school and then had some standing when I became captain of cricket and lacrosse. Then after I left I went to Reading University to read Agriculture and Dairying and miraculously I was top in some exams. When the news reached Miss Willis, she announced in the Dining Room at breakfast that Mary Norman had come top of a university exam and the school must have a holiday to celebrate. She always had time to listen to one's troubles, to comfort, to advise, to stiffen one up or smooth one down, and always with humour – so essential – and wisdom.

Mary Sellar (Norman, 1929)

[Mary Norman went on to found a Downe dynasty. Her daughter is Diane Dennis (Sellar, 1952), her grand-daughter is Katherine Dennis (1974), and her great-grand-daughter is Natalia Colombani (1998).

It was May 1928 and I was thirteen years old. My days of lonely education with a governess were over and I was thrilled to be going to Downe. I was put on the slow train, the Settle line from Carlisle to St Pancras which stopped at Carnforth to pick up several girls from the Lake District. We wore thick purple coats and the hated purple felt hats which sat on our heads like pudding basins. Trunks had been sent in advance, and arriving at Downe we were always met by Miss Willis who gave us a glass of milk.

Rosemary Powell (James, 1932)

Sleeping arrangements

Integration between all ages in the school was the basis of Miss Willis's sleeping arrangements. Gillian Hulbert (Savory, 1962) reports the way things were in her day: 'The first thing to be done on arrival was to find out where and with whom you were sleeping. There were no 'houses' as today, but we were divided between East and West, Hall Rooms, Top, Middle, and Bottom South, and the treat of Ancren Gate with cocoa in the evenings away in the woods at the top of Redshute Hill. Nor did you sleep divided by years; each room had a mixture of years with a senior girl as head of room, and we were further divided into early and late beds. As an early bed, the thing to be was "an early bed in a late bedroom". This meant that you had to be in bed by 8.30, but your light did not go out until 9.30 when the late beds had to be in bed. You officially had a bath every other night, but in practice could usually wangle it so that you bathed every night by sharing someone else's water. There were no showers.'

Belinda Eve (Stobart, 1954), along with several others, recalls the strange custom of the 'sleeping list': 'A major excitement towards the end of each term! Each Senior was allowed to ask one of the juniors to 'sleep' with her the next term, and for a couple of weeks or so there seemed to be no other topic of conversation. Books were kept, gossip on who were the front-runners to be asked, when and where it would happen. Spies were set! It seems incredible now, and we were so naïve. But we loved it, and we hated the Med when she abolished it.'

When Miss Farr introduced the House system, sleeping arrangements were by year group, with girls sharing rooms with others in their year. The practice soon evolved of girls being allowed to ask, at the end of their first term, to share bedrooms with one or more of their friends. The Housemistresses did their best to accommodate these requests and each girl normally found herself with at least one of her chosen companions. This system continues to this day.

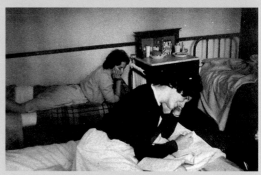

Views of bedrooms: the Big Room, top, now Aisholt Common Room; Hall Rooms in 1961, right; a bedroom probably in West in the 1950s, bottom

I went to Downe in 1920 when I was thirteen. My sister had been there for two years already. It seemed a long way to go, all the way to Kent (we lived in Edinburgh), but Olive Willis was a distant cousin of our father's and he thought he would give her help with the school by sending his two daughters there.

I got a stripe for leaving hair in my brush in a bag in the Boot Room. I appealed against this as the hair in the brush was black and curly and my hair was red and straight. So the stripe was removed. My second term I found I was in a small two-bedded room with a girl I didn't like and she didn't like me either, so we went straight to OW and said we didn't like each other and *must* we share a room. She was very kind and the other girl was moved. I stayed there and a girl who had also been new the term before moved in. We became great friends and remained so all our school days, and I was one of her bridesmaids later on.

Katharine McCulloch
(Inglis, 1925)

Meals and food

As with sleeping arrangements, Miss Willis wanted integration within the whole school and so initiated the system whereby meals were taken in mixed groups of ages from the top of the school to the bottom, and including staff members. Each group was allocated to an individual table, presided over by a member of staff, and was then moved on every few days to a different table. Polite general conversation was expected and silence was considered rude, so Downe girls acquired the often lifelong habit of being able to chat inanely about almost anything. They were also taught never to ask for anything for themselves at mealtimes. 'Do you want the salt?' meant that the questioner did want the salt, so the question was returned and the salt passed over.

The problem with the seating arrangements was that some of the tables seated fewer diners and sometimes a member of staff would arrive for a meal unexpectedly, so an unfortunate junior girl could find herself displaced and then had to 'wander' – find a place at another table. There was always a place, but finding and asking for it – 'May I wander?' – was less than pleasant for shy new girls. Alicia Russell (Eustace, 1934) writes: 'My first week my cousin said "Go and find your table and if there's no room ask to wander." Miss Willis said Grace and I was left standing. "What are you doing, child? Find a place." Well, one appeared.'

There are mixed memories of the quality of food at Downe. Elizabeth Dickson (1952) recalls: 'For the survivor of institutional catering devised from ration books, meals at Downe tasted delicious. Generous helpings too. For breakfast good fresh coffee was served, then after cornflakes we ate crisp fried bread – which we sometimes spread with marmalade – and fried egg, sausage, and bacon. Beetroot featured large, often on Sundays in a white béchamel sauce with rather dubious mutton, or with bottled Heinz salad cream with salad in

The original Dining Room, now the Common Room, above, and one of the original kitchens, below

Downe for virtually nothing, and never said a word. At this same time in the 1930s, when refugees from Nazism began to arrive in Britain, several Jewish couples were welcomed to Downe and their children received a free education.

The principles upon which Miss Willis had founded and built her school were now well established. Her open-armed embrace of change, her dislike of rigidity and closed minds, her deep and discerning interest in all her pupils, her kindness and generosity – all are attested time and time again. Of one highly intelligent but rebellious girl, she wrote (to the girl's mother): 'If ever a child was born to annoy its teachers, that was X. One loves her dearly and curses her heartily, for if she can be late, offhand, or "missing when wanted", she is. . . . She is extraordinarily well and strong, and at the slightest provocation her hair comes straggling down. But how I shall miss her when it is all tidied away and respectable, and there is no flint for my steel!' Another pupil found herself assigned to a bedroom with a girl whom she feared, and went to

summer. Midweek lunch offered a challenging meat hash concoction in gravy, known as Hedgehog. Puddings were a variety of stodge, or stewed fruit, with big white jugs of Bird's custard.'

Gillian Hulbert (Savory, 1962) remembers 'popular dishes given names such as bunny balls (rice and sultanas), cow cake (flapjacks), and bull cake (flapjacks with dates), while dead man's leg is better left undescribed.' Caroline Perkins (McCutcheon, 1967) adds to the list: baby's bottom – pink blancmange; dirty baby's bottom – chocolate blancmange; frog spawn – tapioca; starvation supper on Sunday nights when the kitchen staff were off duty, consisting of one or two slices of cold streaky bacon with a tomato and a banana. Mary Murphy (Pierce, 1970) adds Padd janes, stewed dried apricots, a name based on the supposed appearance of the loos ('janes' at Downe) at Paddington Station.

These mealtime arrangements persisted until the mid-1990s when a cafeteria system was introduced. There were several reasons for the change: increased numbers at the school meant that formal meals, with the whole school seated together, were no longer possible; new Health and Safety regulations did away with the system whereby meals were served from service points at each table, where the food could not be kept at the correct temperature; and there was an increasing need to provide more choices, particularly vegetarian options.

Formal dining in the 1980s, left, and self-service in the 1990s, below

The new system had its advantages; but one notable disadvantage was that it was no longer possible to have 'Notices' at the end of lunch. This was the useful system that had prevailed for the whole of the school's time at Cold Ash whereby at the end of the meal the presiding mistress on the High would call out 'Are there any Notices?' and the Seniors, each positioned at one of the Dining Room pillars, would read out staff announcements, games results, meetings, and any other business.

Weekends

An article in an early school magazine describes a typical intervention by Miss Willis to rescue a wet Saturday from its gloom: 'Saturday May 13th was a horribly wet day, and we were gloomily anticipating games in the gym when Miss Willis suddenly appeared and announced that a competition would be held that evening between the different dormitories, as to which should present the best "turn" in a performance composed of their united efforts.' The result was two ballets, two sets of historical scenes, a 'Back to the Land' song, a skit, and a 'cinema' (presumably a shadow play).

Twenty years later, as Mary Midgley (Scrutton, 1937) writes, Miss Willis was equally watchful: 'I particularly remember one wet Saturday afternoon in my second term when I and a couple of equally grubby friends were standing by the cloakroom wondering dismally what we could do, and she leaned out of her study window and called us to come up. Trouble, we thought, clattering miserably upstairs. But in fact she read Browning to us. It was the first I had heard of Browning, and I was absolutely enchanted. I couldn't understand it all, and got hold of a copy soon after to make it all out. But the wonderful impression of complicated wickedness that she gave, the extraordinary variety her voice was capable of, impressed me immensely. What a way for her to spend her Saturday afternoon.'

Rowena Altham (Portal, 1949) remembers 'those unpromising weekends with rain driving horizontally, making outdoor activity impossible, when Miss Willis or Miss Medley would tap at a glass during Saturday lunch and announce that one class would be responsible for the evening's entertainment. These were called "Penny Readings" and a variety show was expected. With no television to compete, we all enjoyed the fun.'

Celia Edey (Green, 1963) writes about weekends during the late 1950s and early 1960s: 'Most of the important things of life at Downe took place at the weekends. Matches, rehearsals, concerts, films, societies, bicycle rides, picnics, house plays, Saturday evening dances (in the Dining Room after supper, dancing with each other and if brave enough with a member of staff!), and most important of all having time just to be with your friends. From Friday evening and throughout Saturday morning we would be frantically debating with our close friends about

Geraldine James's quotation (in the brochure and chapter 3) sums up so well what so many of us thought. A great deal was expected from each one of us, and we were enabled to give it. I owe my career in archaeology to Olive Willis's interest in new discoveries and her sending the Sixth Form history class off to Queen Anne's to hear Sir Leonard Woolley's first lecture on his discovery of evidence for an enormous flood at Ur in Iraq, and then discussions in scripture classes on the historical value of Genesis.

Girl Guides and Rangers meant weekends camping and building huts in the woods. Ascension Day's whole holiday meant bicycling in threes anywhere except Newbury and freedom for exploring the countryside, or games, or 'doing nothing'. But we were always made aware of our luck and the problems all over the world.

Rachel Maxwell-Hyslop (Clay, 1931)

where we would "bag" for the weekend – a music cell? a sofa in the Gallery? one of the attic rooms in Top Top South? a space in junior library? Decision taken, one of us (depending on our timetables and where our last forty was) would be deputed, as soon as last bell sounded on Saturday morning, to rush to our chosen spot and scatter belongings to claim the space, which would then become our home base for the weekend. Once "bagged" a space was sacrosanct – woe betide anyone trying to take over or impinge on it!

'There we would camp, knowing exactly where our closest friends would be when we returned from an away lacrosse match, or came in from a long bicycle ride (not allowed to cross the A4), or between tea and Chapel. And of course it was from there that we trooped to "temps", that Downe idiosyncrasy whereby at 3pm every Saturday and Sunday, every girl had to line up to have her temperature taken. Saturday evenings were the moment for "home clothes" and special supper. And afterwards a film, a concert, a house play, a lecture – sometimes fascinating, sometimes boring – in the Concert Hall. The staff would sit on the old wooden chairs made for the nuns who had lived there when Downe was a convent. They were made to measure and the staff chose one to fit them – long-legged, short-legged, tall, thin, fat, tiny.

'It was at our temporary "homes" that the Sunday morning letters to our parents were written, where confidences were exchanged, where tuck was eaten, and plots hatched. Where rainy afternoons were happily spent with no hint of homesickness while surrounded by friends. Then Sunday evenings brought the dismantling of our space, and with it that "Sunday evening feeling". But never mind, only four and a half days before we need to start debating next weekend's plan!'

Because of my eyesight I had not been allowed to read or write for a year. But I never got behind during that year because the staff all volunteered to do my prep under my dictation, or read what had to be read. I have a memory of the gym mistress, Miss Charteris, a large person in a short tunic, sitting on the floor in one of the music rooms while I dictated my French prep and going over it, telling her to make sure all the nouns and adjectives agreed with one another and the verbs were in the right tense. Due to the concerted (out of hours) efforts of the staff I was able to do School Certificate at the last minute, which was useful for getting me into Oxford. I don't think many schools would have pulled all together in that way for one pupil.

Nancy Hoare (1934)

The clubs we ran in the evenings were outstandingly good: the history, English, and philosophical ones I particularly remember. We learned to write papers and read them out. At the time of one of the General Elections we ran a mock debate, good practice for any of us interested in national and world politics. We also ran (under the supervision of Jean Rowntree) a monthly newspaper, written by us and duplicated by her. The articles were concocted from ones in *The Times*, the *Manchester Guardian* (as it was then), and the *New Statesman*. It sold for 6d and was called *The Times Explained*.

Judith Hubback (Williams, 1934)

Miss Willis to plead for a change. 'Instead of biting my head off, she took me into her confidence and said, "Her bark is worse than her bite, and you will do each other a lot of good." Needless to say, the person in question has been my one remaining friend of those years ever since.'

Independence of mind and mental flexibility were encouraged. A School Certificate examiner complained that Downe House girls gave their own opinions in their papers instead of quoting authorities; an Oxford tutor noticed that they were particularly receptive to ideas, even when they were less well equipped factually than the products of some other schools. That their school had educated them as persons as well as instructing their minds was the comment of

43

44

another teacher who had met a number of them as students.

Olive Willis's one criticism of her successor was, 'She doesn't like my stupid ones.' And indeed she consistently encouraged the less academically able to flourish where they could. In her own words, 'I felt that it was very important to develop self-confidence in children even if there were not many signs of progress. Some sense of achievement was necessary, and if lessons were not satisfactory, then some other activity must be found in which the unacademic girl could excel.' Accordingly, she gave leave in the middle of term to one girl who was slow at her books to go and milk her prize cow at the Royal Show.

RIGHT: **The meditation chairs in use**

I think Miss Willis was a wonderful headmistress, as she made everyone feel wanted and important – even if they were untidy and bumptious like me. At my previous school I had enjoyed rebelling, so was somewhat taken aback to find virtually no rules to break at Downe. Miss Willis said that rules were made to be broken, so it was best to have as few as possible. I finally ended up as Head Senior – on the 'set a thief to catch a thief' principle – but before that I certainly collected more stripes than most people. Therefore I spent many a Saturday afternoon learning Shakespeare and various poems, or in the summer pulling thistles.

Jill Lewis (Bradfield, 1937)

I arrived at the beginning of the autumn term in 1933 extremely shy and nervous, having spent some years at a small boarding school run by a sadist, where new girls were beaten and humiliated. I could hardly believe the difference at Downe where everybody was so kind and friendly. My worst memories of Downe were of the cold, resulting in chilblains on fingers and toes throughout the winter. The happiest days were what were called 'sun holidays', declared if it was unusually nice weather in the winter. At ten o'clock word went round the school and lessons would cease for the day. We collected sandwiches and drinks and were unleashed into the country lanes in groups of three or more. It was extremely exciting and made us blissfully happy. We were privileged to enjoy such freedom. I remember visiting the old bowl man at Bucklebury Common and still have some of the bowls he'd made.

Pearl Brewis (Beaumont-Thomas, 1938)

She was unpredictable too. On one occasion, in front of the entire school assembled in the gym, she hitched up her skirt and scratched her thigh. As the school gasped she said merely: 'Yes, my dears, that's what *you* do. I thought you wouldn't like it.' Another time she handed over a banana to a girl whose shoes were looking the worse for wear, with the words 'You eat the banana and rub the skin on your shoes.' Another recollection is, 'We were much more likely to be reprimanded for lack of initiative than for any rule-breaking.' And yet again, 'Girls, you must understand that if I am very cross with you it is because I can see a solution for improvement. But if I refer to you as "My

I think one should be able to say of a really good school that one was happy there, but not happiest. After all, your school is supposed to help you to grow up. . . . We were militant about lots of things . . . and that, I think, was one of the very good things about Downe. Your opinions, however violent and immature they may have been, were taken seriously, though not necessarily agreed with. That seems to me to be exactly as it should be; after all, however young you are, it does matter what you think.

It was very fashionable to be what might be called 'a character'. It was high praise to say that somebody was 'rather eccentric'. We looked upon absence of mind and unpunctuality as proofs of intellect. (I myself, was, and always have been, pathologically punctual, but I used to force myself to be late from time to time, lest I should be suspected of dullness and conventionality.) We entertained our parents with stories, some of them true, of the curious behaviour of the staff at Downe. We told them that Miss Nickel slept in a bath, with a pile of books for a pillow . . . that Madame was wont to lean over the Gallery of the Dining Room dangling some fearful object (say, a suspender) crying ''Oo is 'e?'' and then, in tones of deepening despair, ''E must be somebody.' We also, so my mother used to assure me, told her that practically everybody in the school whom we knew and liked was 'quite mad'. In her innocence she believed this, and formed an impression of classes of amiable mental defectives. It must have surprised her that most of us passed our examinations, and that the behaviour of our friends when they came to stay in the holidays was perfectly normal. . . . We certainly did our best to avoid becoming what we imagined the average schoolgirl to be. 'What was it like?' we used to ask the lacrosse team, returning from some match at another school. 'Oh, very *schooly*,' the answer would come, and there could not be stronger condemnation than that.

Jacobine Sackville-West (Menzies Wilson, 1938)

darling child" I have reached the point where only "Loving you better" may create a miracle.'

Miss Willis's dislike of rigid divisions into houses or year groups, and her desire to encourage relationships across the whole school, resulted in a custom that persisted at Downe until modern Health and Safety legislation necessitated change. This was the procedure whereby pupils were put into groups of nine or ten for meals – one or two from each year, headed by a member of the Sixth Form. These groups remained together for two or three weeks and moved every few days to a different table where a new member of staff presided. It was necessary to converse with each other and

with the staff and to keep everyone engaged and entertained. This had its disadvantages – notably the much-disliked need sometimes to 'wander' – but it inculcated conversational skills that, for better or worse, often lasted a lifetime. As Priscilla Napier (Hayter, 1926) wrote in the *Scrap-Book*: 'Making conversation became, in many of us, an ineradicable nervous habit. To this day, the briefest lull at a luncheon or dinner party is instantly filled by me with remarks of an inanity which startles

'A mystery and a miracle'. What a wonderful and apt title. It is true to say that scarcely a day goes by when I do not think of Downe. I was one of the extremely fortunate ones – to be there with Olive Willis who touched our lives with her influence. I was desperately homesick for three weeks at the beginning of every term, but when I settled down all I wanted to do was play games. I got into the first lacrosse XII when I was twelve, and I got my colours for lacrosse and gym, but I think I was an academic failure. My Latin report one term was 'Diana sits up like a ramrod and takes absolutely nothing in.' Fortunately, my parents were not so bothered about academic success but more about other aspects of education. That was the greatest thing about Downe House. I remember so well that Miss Willis would suddenly appear in our form room at the beginning of a forty and give us a talk on things like 'influence' or 'pronunciation': 'girl' must be 'gairl', 'laundry' must be 'londry', and so on. I remember climbing the trees in the woods and how you graduated from the 'small girl's hole' to the 'big girl's hole'. These were circles made by misshapen branches and very difficult to get through. You were no-one until you had done the 'big girl's hole'. Do they do it now, I wonder? They certainly don't swim with frogs and slime in the swimming bath and get streptococcal throats, as we did.

Diana Gifford Mead (Collins, 1938)

Downe House, Cold Ash, Newbury.

The swimming pool

Medical matters

The health and well-being of girls at a boarding school are and have always been paramount. Many of the recollections of medical matters in the old days are humorous, though there are also more serious memories of illnesses and (rarely) a death. Medical issues were always a high priority, but the emphases have moved with the times and the facilities now available are of a very high standard indeed and embrace all aspects of health, traditional and alternative, with the aim of caring for all the girls in a holistic, non-judgmental way.

Rosemary Tredgold (Walker, 1957) remembers the rituals and rules that attended matters of health: 'Temperatures were taken every day for the first three weeks of term and then every weekend. Did they really think we brought such illnesses from home? We wondered too if the weekend queues were a way of ensuring we didn't stray too far. Then there was the ritual of "signing the board". It was considered wrong for menstruating young women to play sport, so those who loved sport and did not want to miss games "signed the board" on Mondays, and those who wanted to miss sport did so on Fridays. Emotional health received less attention. Many of us were initially very homesick and we learnt to cut off emotional responses. When one of our form died during our time at school, this could only be denied.'

Rowena Altham (Portal, 1949): 'Only girls with clear health certificates were accepted for the new term. There were no jabs, no antibiotics. One ticked off mumps, whooping cough, measles, chickenpox with relief as there would then be

even my children. Into the silence of any difficult situation my voice can be heard uncontrollably pointing out how late the daffodils are this year. This is a grave disadvantage, and it has long been my ambition to award a valuable annual prize at

immunity. Epidemics would overflow the San, chilblains on hands and feet were winter standards. . . . I spent three weeks in the San with measles, but had to be moved because the girl sharing the room was so ill her mother was sent for, and moved in. Mercifully, she pulled through.'

Sister Kite is a fond memory for many. Susan Schanche (Gaddum, 1947) speaks for many when she recalls the rituals of reporting sick. 'Sister had three possible responses. The worst was, "There's nothing wrong with you," and the only thing was to walk away in shame as a "well" person who had tried to fool Sister. The second best response was, "I think we will have to send you to the San," when we were really ill. The third and best response was, "Go and have a bath and come back." This meant that one could jump to the front of the queue, have a lovely hot bath, and then go back to Sister's office for a wonderful hot lemon drink. Real luxury!'

Memories from the different generations demonstrate the importance of the 'San sisters' in the life of the school. Many of them oversaw several generations of girls, and some of the remedies prescribed remain part of the health armoury of Old Seniors in later life. One such remedy originated with Sister Hunter, who was convinced of the efficacy of Guinness in almost all situations!

A long-standing 'San sister' was Sister Austin, who ran the San for many years until her retirement in 1997, with the assistance of Sister Clouting and Sister Britz. Now called the Medical

At the end of October 1931 I suddenly became very ill with a bone disease called osteomyelitis and was whisked to a nursing home in Reading for the first of what turned out to be many operations on my legs. My mother's acute anxiety was shared by Miss Willis; a cousin of mine had died from measles contracted when at Downe. Was history repeating itself? Apart from the acute pain involved, I was miserable at missing school and my friends, and was much cheered when a coach returning from a successful match stopped outside the nursing home and everyone waved. When I had to have a night nurse, I asked whether I could have Sister Kite as she had no patients at the time. Sister duly arrived and in fact stayed for the next five months, later looking after me at home until I was able to be up on crutches. I returned to Downe – still on crutches – in the middle of the following summer term. Here Miss Willis's genius for flexibility came into play. The classrooms were reorganised so that all my lessons would take place in E, and I wouldn't have to negotiate the long slippery steps down to the classrooms near the gym. All the staff cooperated and gave me extra coaching too as I had missed so much of the year.

Delle Fletcher (Chenevix-Trench, 1933)

47

Centre, with Sister Clouting in charge, the high-level medical facilities are housed in new, purpose-built accommodation in the grounds. Medical help of all sorts can be found there, with many specialists on call – counsellors, physiotherapists, chiropodists, and so on – and highly-qualified medical staff always available. There have always been school doctors too, visiting from their local practices. Mention is made elsewhere of Dr Bradley-Moore (sister-in-law of Alice Moore, a very early pupil), who was the school doctor for many years in the 1940s and 1950s, and more recently Drs West, Robertson, and Morgan have given long service to the school, on call as needed and coming in regularly to run surgeries.

Downe for the most consistently silent girl.'

From the beginning Olive Willis had been determined that her girls should be encouraged to take an adult interest in world affairs; parochialism always irked her. Accordingly, when the Second

World War started, she ensured that they were kept abreast of news of the war by being allowed to listen to the radio news every day, and when invasion seemed imminent she ensured that every pupil had a bag containing iron rations and a little

**Olive Willis with
Old Seniors**

Reposing on the lawn outside the Dining Room was a potty which had been thrown out of one of the bedrooms earlier. You can imagine the consternation at breakfast – who? However, the culprit confessed that morning. But she had the last laugh as her parents were rather surprised to find on the school bill among the 'extras': one large teacup, 2/6d.

Sheila Farrar (1940)

Once I received a letter from a boyfriend who swore particular devotion and wanted to come to see me at school as he was in a bad state. I showed Miss Willis his letter and asked if he could be allowed to have tea in the grounds and talk. She read the letter and agreed. 'I completely trust you,' she said. So he came and we had tea, and afterwards he wrote again thanking Miss Willis and me for giving him courage and a new faith in himself.

Josephine Street (Dane, 1940)

money. The spectacular white of the buildings was camouflaged, and Miss Nickel built a long, dank tunnel to act as an air raid shelter. Black-out was achieved initially by the use of dark blue bulbs which, one pupil of the time recalls, put paid completely to any idea of breaking the rules about reading in bed.

But at the same time Miss Willis was not about to deprive her girls of their childhood, and she made sure that teaching and leisure activities continued as normally as possible. The war was not allowed to disrupt musical and theatrical performances which, as the school magazines of the time record, were livelier than ever. Those who were there at the time have vivid memories of the visits made by Dame Myra Hess, who was a friend of Marjorie Gunn, and Mr Sharwood Smith continued to put on Classical dramas, including his own translation of the *Women of Trachis*.

The 'Spees' were another distraction: pupils of Queen's Gate school in London, evacuated from dangerous London to Downe owing to the friendship between Miss Willis and their Headmistress,

Miss Spalding. It soon became apparent that the two schools were like chalk and cheese in almost every respect, and activities were conducted separately, though the Queen's Gate girls were invited to the musical and dramatic events.

The inevitable tragedies of wartime hit Downe, and Miss Willis sometimes had the melancholy task of passing on the news of the death of a father or a brother. Closer to home, Miss Heather was found to be suffering from bone cancer in 1943, and died just before the beginning of the autumn term in that year. This was a crippling

loss, and the end of thirty-six years of partnership and friendship. It came, too, at a time when Olive Willis was beginning to plan her own retirement and a change in the status of the school.

Up till now Downe House had been a private company; now, in 1944, it was to become a public body, with a Board of Governors. And a year later Miss Willis announced that she would be retiring at the end of the summer term of 1946, though she would remain on the Board of Governors and also intended to keep Hill House as her own residence. This, however, caused a difficulty for her

So cold at night that I put most of my clothes for the morning into my bed, to keep them as warm as me. In summer, when the rose garden was all flower and scent, I had extra Latin there, in a sort of gazebo, with Mr Sharwood-Smith (right), retired headmaster of Newbury Grammar School. I had failed the Latin School Certificate I needed for Oxford, so he coached me (and someone else – who?). He read Lucretius out loud to us, and his voice has never left me – a rhythm and throatiness that conveyed to us the value of the mysterious language we were trying to learn. When pleased, Mr Sharwood-Smith had a characteristic gesture – he would rub his hair forward from behind his ears. I was no good at games, but I turned out to be good at umpiring – valuable in later life, as it taught me to project my voice across wide spaces, in meetings where most women are inaudible.

I remember the arrival of Ruth Moses, refugee with her mother and sister from Germany where her father and brothers had vanished into the Nazi hell. She taught German and not only got me through School Certificate in one term but gave me long-lasting elements of Goethe. Later I lived with her mother and sister in Oxford. It was wartime and they gave me – goy that I was – their bacon ration.

Miss Willis: amazing woman. She knew each of the 140-odd of us, inside, outside, where we had come from, where we were going. Lovingly. If she had been a man, she would have made a wonderful bishop. She did wear purple taffeta. Then there were Jean Rowntree, Brenda Sanderson, Mamie Poore: wonderful teachers all and intellectually glamorous, worldly in the best sense. JR vanished in the summer of 1939, into Czechoslovakia I think, and brought back to England people at risk. Mamie Poore's clothes were wonderfully glamorous – almost theatrical. The Hut was a small wooden building in the woods, where the three of them may have lived – I don't know – but they certainly worked and entertained there.

Elizabeth Kennet (Adams, 1941)

50

As a twelve-year-old arriving at Downe in September 1935, I was greeted by a vision that has never faded: Miss Willis descending from on high to welcome a newcomer, in a flutter of beautiful scarves and draperies, with outstretched arms, a luminous smile, and the delighted cry, 'So there you are, my dears.' I was consumed by reverence and awe. My mother addressed this snowy-haired presence as 'Cousin Olive', which was reassuring. Perhaps it was the impact of that initial meeting that made me feel that I was not just a member of a school but also a guest in the house of a gracious hostess, whose very presence, irrespective of what she said and did, drove me to try to please her. There always remained an undercurrent of endeavour to live up to Miss Willis's hopes for us. The end-of-term 'jaw' fuelled this aspiration, for although she would make us face our perceived shortcomings, there invariably followed an encouraging indication of what we might become. However, 'becoming' was not, to Miss Willis, an end in itself. She taught us that we were put in the world with opportunities to be of service, and such talents as we had were fostered to that end, whether we were artistic, academic, or possessed of more mundane abilities.

Marigold Freeman-Attwood (Philips, 1942)

When I arrived just before the war started, in 1938, my first concern was that there was already an Elizabeth Young, so what was I to be called? Had I a home nickname? Yes – 'Buff'. But alas, the existing Elizabeth Young was already 'Buffie'. What about my second name? Mary – also no good as the lady gardener was Mary Young. So I became M E (definitely not 'Emmy') and am still M E to my Downe friends to this day. I don't think wartime affected us hugely and we were probably more sheltered than I realised. But we did have the obligatory red line painted round the baths so that you used two – or was it four? – inches of water only. And because the ringing of church bells was to be the sign of invasion, I never rang the Chapel bell.

M E Young (1942)

What was valuable, I think, was the great feeling of natural unity and common purpose during the war. With the various shortages of things such as petrol and travelling facilities, there were no such things as half terms and scarcely any outings, with the result that it was a very close-knit community. The sleeping and eating arrangements assisted in this, and friendships covered a very wide age range. We were really very dependent on our own resources and there were constant plays, concerts, and choral recitals. We had a few short air raids and a number of air raid practices in the underground tunnel . . . and we had a current events lecture every week, and Miss Willis announced any major developments in the progress of the war in the Dining Room at meal times. On Sunday nights when there was an extended nine o'clock news the Seniors were all invited to the Drawing Room to listen to the news and discuss it afterwards. Miss Willis's advice during the 'jaws' was extraordinarily perceptive . . . though I did think that her advice on matrimony – 'to refuse the first seven' – was a bit hazardous!

Avril Wotherspoon (Edwards, 1945)

In September 1939 Miss Willis allowed a few younger sisters and some day girls to be admitted. I was one of those lucky ones, and became a boarder in January 1940. Some memories: building houses in the woods; attending current affairs talks with maps so that we could see how the war was progressing; going to a hospital near Hermitage in a group from Choral to sing to the wounded (those poor men – how they must have hated it!); Hare and Hounds on snowy days in winter and snow on our beds if you slept under a window (which always had to be open). The Military Exercise one Sunday morning – looking out and seeing that either the French Canadians or the Americans had 'captured' the school. We were set free in due course by the other side, but were still allowed to go out in threes during the occupation, gaining quite a store of chewing gum and magazines. Great fun!

Cynthia Taylor (Acland, 1945)

M y only claim to fame is that I was the first day girl! In 1940 my mother went to Miss Willis and asked if I could be a day girl as we lived on Bucklebury Common. 'What an interesting idea,' said Miss Willis. 'Shall we say £10 a term?' So started my undistinguished but very happy career at Downe. Later I boarded when my mother realised bombs were not necessarily going to kill us all.
Susan Marsden-Smedley (King, 1946)

assumed successor, Brenda Sanderson, who had been a member of the history staff since 1932. She was concerned that her own position would be made untenable by the proximity of the school's charismatic founder, and she told the Board that she could not accept the post under those conditions. Olive Willis was predictably hurt by what she saw as a lack of confidence in her ability to maintain an appropriate distance, and offered to give up Hill House; but the Board were unwilling to jettison the value of her continued connection with the school and refused her offer.

Miss Sanderson accordingly left for another headship, and the post was advertised. Nancy Medley, who had been one of the English staff since 1935, was persuaded to apply and was duly appointed. She took over as Headmistress in January 1947.

Olive Willis continued to live at Hill House until her death in 1964, and each year invited the new girls to tea. But she also had a house in Italy, a cottage in the Quantocks, and a flat in London, and she divided her time between all these residences. Indeed, as Sheila Bateman (Gamble, 1954) recounts: 'Her neighbours in Tedworth Square were amused to see successions of elegantly dressed women checking their hair and make-up in car mirrors and generally ensuring that their appearance was up to scratch before ringing her doorbell.' Her influence persisted!

Wartime memories

Hannelore Maier (1940) was sent to Downe from Germany in 1937. Her parents were anxious about the developing crisis in Europe and were keen to take the chance of their daughter receiving an education elsewhere. But during her first year at the school her father tragically killed himself and Hannelore returned to Germany to collect her mother and brother and take them to England. She was only able to organise papers for her brother and so they returned to England without their mother, who was later sent to Auschwitz. She remembers Miss Willis as 'formidable, but very kind and interested. She arranged for me to spend Sundays with two German teachers from the school so that I would not be lonely. I was very withdrawn and quite shy, but I learned to speak English in one term. . . . Downe gave me an extremely good education, but I was very traumatised by what was going on in Germany as well as the separation from my family, so I learnt but did not necessarily involve myself in school life.'

Elizabeth Jackson (Hall, 1943) writes: 'Early on, I presume in 1940 or 1941, the Air Ministry decreed that the criss-cross paving between the Cloisters was being used by the Luftwaffe as a night point of reference, as it stood out for miles around in the moonlight. So the whole school turned out and dragged pine branches cut from the surrounding woods to cover all the paving. I never heard exactly what happened, but a week later we were told that the ruse had not been successful and the whole lot had to be dragged away again. I can only presume that the dark pine against the grass was almost as obvious as the paving. My selfish reason for remembering this

Going to war, 1939; one of the few photographs from the war years

particular episode is that I lost my fountain pen in the woods and some important exam was imminent. In the pre-biro days that was disastrous!'

Margaret Payne remembers the shock she felt when 'in 1944 we woke up and looked out of the window, to see soldiers and vehicles everywhere under the pine trees around the school. They were Canadian troops *en route* to the coast waiting for the start of D-Day. You can imagine our excitement, but it soon waned when we were confined to the Cloisters until they moved away.'

Primrose Henderson (Forrest, 1945) writes: 'One very clear memory was the night of June 6th 1944 when we were woken by the constant roar of aeroplanes overhead, many towing gliders. It was a staggering sight and seemed to go on for hours.

Heads were hanging out of windows on all sides. Something important had to be happening. At breakfast Miss Willis told us that the invasion of Europe had begun and she hoped we had had some sleep during the night. During the next days we were to watch trains in the valley with Red Crosses painted on the roof bringing back the wounded. Indeed a worrying sight for girls with fathers or brothers at the front.'

Jennifer Hollings (Hutt, 1947) writes: 'I think we were amazingly sheltered both from the awful realities of war and from the logistical problems there must have been in keeping the school going. We played at being super-patriotic: gathered sphagnum moss for field dressings in Palmer's Woods, tried to identify aircraft, picked rose hips for vitamin C, called our pets Winston, and it was all rather fun. We knitted for the troops too: clever people made socks with beautifully turned heels, middling knitters were assigned balaclava helmets, and complete duffers got to do scarves.

I have been describing trivialities; our lives at Downe seemed perfectly normal at the time, and our immediate concerns were probably very similar to those of today – friendships, exams, societies, games. One of our form was a refugee from Czechoslovakia where her father was in a concentration camp but somehow we never talked about this. The war did break into our insular lives at times when Miss Willis wanted to see someone in her study and we all achingly knew that a father or a brother had been killed. And on D-Day the throb of many planes woke us before the first bell and continued all day long above the Cloisters and the lily pond and the whole of southern England.'

Then there were 'the Spees'. Miss Spalding – known as 'Spee', hence the nickname for her pupils – was the Headmistress of Queen's Gate School in London and an acquaintance of Olive Willis. So when war became imminent in the summer of 1939 it was decided that Queen's Gate would be evacuated to Downe House. Having to cram another eighty people into already squeezed accommodation was a challenge, particularly since staff and pupils at the incoming school were used to much more luxurious conditions than Downe offered even in peacetime.

'We were asked to welcome them,' wrote Ruth Aspinall in the *Scrap-Book*, 'in a manner fitting to hosts, and I believe that we were friendly enough. But somehow our very first view of them in the Dining Room, their tidiness and apparent sophistication, gave us a shock from which we never recovered. . . . At the time neither I nor any of the rest of us realised that to the uninitiated a djibbah might seem a very strange garment indeed, or that to Miss Spalding's girls – so much in the minority, and moreover used to living in their own homes, for it was a day school – our noise and abandoned cheerfulness might appear boisterous and alarming.'

The two schools and the two headmistresses were so different that they could never have been successfully merged, so all lessons and other activities were separate. As two of the Queen's Gate girls (Elizabeth and Ann Rucker) recall, 'There were two separate Girl Guide Companies and two sections to the Girls' Training Corps, even though the latter were instructed by the same person, who came on different days. The two schools competed at games with QG usually being beaten, though we did succeed in winning at tennis as two of our girls were extremely competent players. We regretted being unable to join in the massed dancing and gym, and would have welcomed taking advantage of the superb music teaching. However, we

appreciated being invited to special concerts and performances, and particularly remember a recital by Dame Myra Hess and a magical performance of *Peer Gynt* in the Cloisters.'

Cherry Palmer has similar memories. 'That first winter was one of the coldest on record, and I so remember walking backwards and forwards between Hill House and the school – the birch trees were magically encased in ice, each separate twig, so that the tinkling in the breeze was like a fairy story. Children don't notice the cold too much but it was the only time I (and many others) had chilblains.'

She remembers Downe House camouflaged in a dirty khaki, with brown paper strips on all the windows in case of bombs, and the Giant's Stride, and music and theatrical performances in the Cloisters. 'It is sad,' she adds, 'looking back on those years, that we didn't mix with the Downes. They thought of us as London snobs, we thought of them as country simpletons – so untrue!'

Sue Woodroffe (Farrer, 1948) still has the letter (see page 53) she wrote in high excitement to tell her mother about the VE day celebrations (and other things): 'Isn't this wonderful! I feel I must put something in my letter as everyone here last night went absolutely wild with excitement. Of course yesterday was a holiday and just after breakfast we all went out to watch the St George's Cross being hoisted on the Chapel tower and then went to buy red white and blue rosettes from Madame. We then had a lovely service in the chapel and afterwards went to look at the flags by the front gate. We had nice picnic lunches and could eat them wherever we liked and at three came in to listen to the Prime Minister. When that was over we went out to Field and gave sports to the village children, said goodbye to them at half past four, had tea, and changed into cotton dresses (I wore your blue one). Then we had chapel during which we listened to the Archbishop of Canterbury. We listened to the king at nine. After supper we all went out to St Peter's Hill where our beacon was going to be lit and as the flames began roaring to the sky we all sang and cheered and made as much noise as we possibly could until it was quite dark and then gradually we saw other beacons lighting up, some over thirty miles away. Then as the flames died down we sang a few more songs and were then shooed to bed by Miss Willis. It was after eleven before we were in bed.

'Now, I have been told that summer tunics don't come for about five or six months after they are ordered so do you think you could write a tactful letter to 'Sheba' and say that I have *got* to have one for Seniors Weekend and also that I have to wear a djibbah and they are *very* hot. Also could you send a few belts as we have to have them for the tunics and a brown one (belt) for Seniors weekend. I wonder whether you could make out a few coupons for an aertex blouse as they are so useful for school.'

Postscript – VE Day remembered fifty years on

In May 1995, in common with the rest of the nation, Downe commemorated the Jubilee of VE day by re-enacting the activities of the pupils fifty years earlier. Girls enthusiastically decorated the buildings with rather unusual red, white, and blue bunting engineered from the contents of their wardrobes and the Sixth Form followed suit with their attire. An authentic lunch in a decorated Dining Room, including spam fritters and Woolton pie, was more reluctantly endured and perhaps accounted for the great welcome given to the picnic tea eaten outside in glorious sunshine later in the day. During lunch and again later, the Wind Band, led by Jack Wilkinson, swung into action with a miscellany of 1940s popular music. Girls had obviously been practising beforehand since many were able to sing along to 'A Nightingale sang in Berkeley Square', 'The White Cliffs of Dover', and many more.

In the evening a moving service was held in Jubilee Hall. This included the observation of the Two Minutes Silence and an address by Jennifer Gosse, who had been a pupil in 1945 and spoke of that time. The celebrations concluded with a large bonfire, lit by Head Senior Mary Rose Gunn dressed as Britannia, which joined the large number of beacons around the country. More community singing rounded off the occasion.

CHAPTER 3

Changing times

OPPOSITE: **The Giant's Stride in use**

58

Taking over the leadership of any institution is a process always fraught with difficulty; but taking over Downe House after forty years of Miss Willis's inspirational and idiosyncratic helmsmanship was never going to be anything but a challenge – and particularly since she was to remain on the Board of Governors and to carry on living, at least some of the time, at Hill House. Moreover, Nancy Medley was a charismatic English teacher – Caroline Ailesbury (Wethered, 1954) remembers her as 'a gaunt, highly intelligent person who made *Paradise Lost* seem fascinating and comprehensible' – and it is likely that her initial reluctance to take over the headship sprang mainly from her desire to continue her teaching commitments to the full.

But take the job on she did, and she remained a highly respected and much admired figure until she died shortly after retiring in 1963. The introduction to the *Magazine* of 1947 expresses her ethos exactly: 'Many of you will doubtless think that this first page should hold a grateful account of the enormous work Miss Willis has done for the last forty years in starting, building up, and firmly establishing as a great Public School this Downe House of ours. That it does not is not because we do not appreciate what she has done, nor because we are not grateful for it; but because there is an old proverb which remarks that one should wait until the entertainment is concluded before praising it. Although Miss Willis now no longer wholly belongs to the school, it still wholly belongs to her, it still has a lien on her affections, it still depends on her wisdom and experience. Only when those things are no longer true will we bring ourselves to look back and count our blessings. Until then we will continue to look forward with courage and confidence: we will not be overshadowed by the greatness of our past, nor fearful of the difficulties of the future, because we know that something so strongly built and so firmly supported can be neither overshadowed nor overcome.'

Miss Medley's first Vice-Principal was Elizabeth Palmer, a great benefactor of the school who had been closely associated with Downe House since 1920, when she joined the school in Kent. She moved with it to Cold Ash and later lived at Fencewood, opposite the school. She joined the office staff during the war before being appointed Vice-Principal and, after she left that post, continued to open her doors at Fencewood to members of staff until she died in 1998, when she left the house to the school. She had previously allowed the school to use part of the house for

Elizabeth Palmer as a pupil in 1920 and in 1996

60

Meetings with 'the Med' were, I hear, terrifying for many, but Patience and I used to vie with each other to make her laugh. She would most engagingly wrinkle up her nose, throw back her head, and, I think, guffaw – or snort. And then one was delighted, even if the actual message of the 'jaw' had been 'Really, Juliet, your exercise books look like a series of crossword puzzles – every other word blotted out.' And, of course, the inevitable verdict – impossible to alter or gainsay – 'could do better'. Oh dear, yes. I know I only worked at what I was good at.

Once – overwhelmed by sheer panic in the middle of the night – I could think of no recourse but Miss Medley who, it was said, hardly slept at all. She answered the door and sat me down kindly in the 'jaw' chair. She warmed up a milky drink for me and asked, 'So you feel you are going mad. What form would your madness take – angry mad? Or melancholy mad?' I thanked her and said 'melancholy mad', with apologies. She reassured me, and advised me on sipping the drink hot and on leaving lights off so as 'not to make an enemy of the dark.' This I don't forget; and even then it struck me how dedicated she was, existing in those two tiny rooms as on the bridge of a ship, responsible for everything – even for soothing my madness. Her death, far too young, was a great sadness to me.

Juliet Rees (Gowan, 1947)

Winter (Lent) term 1947 was Miss Medley's first term as Head, so there were two terms when everyone was exceptionally well-behaved – Miss Willis's last and Miss Medley's first. It was also the exceptionally cold term when the whole country ran out of coal. Every year we were used to face flannels beside open bedroom windows freezing at night, but this winter we had to wrap ourselves in dressing gowns and eiderdowns under the sheets. I had spent the Christmas holidays in Vienna, so I had skiing trousers in my school luggage. I asked Miss Medley for permission to wear them, and as Sister Kite knew I suffered from chilblains (did not we all?) I was allowed. Immediately everybody else wrote home asking for trousers until, when one girl appeared in her mother's elegant leopard-skin trousers, Miss Medley said 'no more!' Luckily it was beginning to thaw a little by then. This was the term when Madame, who supervised the second-hand school uniforms and had for years had racks of unpopular purple wool overcoats, suddenly found them selling like hot cakes.

Alison Mitchell (1947)

staff accommodation, and she also gave marvellous dinners for individual staff members, where they could relax and enjoy convivial evenings around the drawing-room fire, away from school routine and well fed by her splendid cook, Shirley.

Under Miss Medley Downe House continued to flourish. School magazines for these years list Old Seniors offered scholarships at the Oxford and Cambridge women's colleges, plays and concerts of all kinds, clubs going strong, lectures and films enjoyed (or sometimes not), sports and games enthusiastically played and followed. The school was well established and successful, and

In retrospect it is not so much the shortage of clothes that appals me but how we must have smelled, for our weekly laundry bag was not allowed to contain more than one set of underwear, one pair of socks, one shirt, and the odd handkerchief; and baths, seldom hot and never deep, were limited to three a week. To brace us we were told that the king had a red line painted round all the baths at Buckingham Palace at the five inch level, but we doubted that he had to share it. Hair washing was limited to once every three weeks except for the very greasies who could do it fortnightly. Nevertheless, I don't remember feeling dirty at the time. What I do remember is feeling cold. Except for a fire in the staff common room there was no heat in the school. None. Yet we idiotically considered it soft, verging on unpatriotic, to wear stockings or long socks. Whenever I have been cold since I tell myself 'not as bad as Downe'.

Jennifer Hollings (Hutt, 1947)

I started at Downe in Lent 1941, aged eight. There was a day girl younger than me but I was the youngest boarder for a long while. Altogether I spent twenty-five terms at Downe. My mother didn't care for her daughter to wear second-hand clothing so she transferred the embroidered section on to a new piece of green curtain material, thus making a new djibbah. But I always felt odd because my djibbah was different to everyone else's and I longed for the faded patched hessian material which others wore.

Jennifer Walker (1949)

Jubilee celebrations in 1957: Miss Medley at the tree planting, right, and Jubilee Hall, below

pupils of the time have fond memories of their Headmistress. Josephine Walker (Holmes, 1963) is typical: 'Looking through my box of things from Downe I was astonished to find a letter from Miss Medley to my mother, written a couple of weeks into my first term and reassuring her that I was all right and surviving. My father had died a few months before, and I expect she was keeping an eye

62

Downe to me spells two things: freedom and friendship. The fact that the school was small meant that you could know everybody, at least by name, and I think I did so through my six years there, except towards the very end. This added to the friendly atmosphere of the place. But of course it was Miss Willis whose breadth of vision and humour made Downe such a haven for free spirits. What other headmistress would have addressed her charges as 'My darling children . . .', or been so sensible, when punishment was inescapable, of making it unforgettably fit the crime? I learned this early on, as a junior with other juniors at Ancren Gate, when a group of us caught reading after lights out had to spend what seemed like a whole night reading, begging to be allowed to go to bed.

I would like to celebrate the memory of those who taught me, some eccentric as well as interesting people whose talents Miss Willis had a knack for attracting, not necessarily great at their subjects, but nevertheless memorable and likeable – and entirely of their time. I have vivid recollections from those long six years, of geography with Miss Croft (I got 2% in the exam) and Miss Bate ('I know I'm an old bear'; one day she broke her pointer through her habit of stretching it round her neck), of history with Miss Lewin and later on with Miss Bewick, dashing in her cloak and always beautiful in make-up, who took the subject away from those terrible green textbooks filled with potted facts, to ideas and ideals and thoughts as excitingly connected as the flow of her joined-up handwriting. Thanks to Miss Barnsley and Miss Medley, lines of Milton and Browning still sound in my memory, and when I was doing Higher Certificate dear Miss Hickson had to mug up the art history and loyally kept one lesson ahead. Music owed a great deal to Miss Read, a brilliant teacher. She was portly, with delicate ankles, and when she sat in one of the high-sided meditation chairs (do they still exist?), the question always was, would she be able to rise to her feet? [Eds: There are a few of the meditation chairs still around in the school (and see page 44).]

Margaret Buxton (Bridges, 1950)

on me, but a two-page, hand-written letter seems to me to be miraculously kind and thoughtful when she must have been so busy.'

In 1957 Downe House celebrated its half century, its Jubilee. Those who left at the end of the summer term in 1952 had started a campaign to raise money for a theatre as a fitting memorial of the first fifty years of the school's life, and fund-raising for this project went on over the next five years. Miss Medley used the *Magazine* of 1956 to record some of the efforts made to raise money: 'bed-making for the lazy, car-cleaning for the affluent, wood-collecting for the fortunate with fireplaces', plus sales and appeals for donations. That year the ground was cleared for what was to become Jubilee Hall, the building of which went on throughout 1957, Jubilee year itself, until it was

When I was asked whether I would prefer to go to Oxford High School or to Downe, they showed me a djibbah. Fatal! I fell in love with it immediately and said 'Downe please'. We loved our djibbahs and Madame, Miss Willis's old French nanny who spoke almost no English, sat in the Gallery mending and patching the backs when the Irish folk weave wore through on school chairs. The Gallery, of course, was above the Dining Room: that beautiful wood-lined room where we all learned to keep the conversation going. My husband says he recognises Downe girls by the way we never let silences develop!

There was another wood-lined room: the Concert Room with its warm acoustics. Tuesday evening is orchestra night and Marjorie Gunn is conducting Haydn or Mozart with the current dog on the rostrum and Mary Young on the double bass. Fiddle lessons were in the adjoining no 15, redolent with Army and Navy Egyptian cigarettes and paraffin stove to thaw chilblained fingers.

The beauty of the place got under one's skin, subliminally. The architecture: cloisters, chapel, lily pond, Greek theatre; the walks in Palmer's woods; the music: Choral singing 'Gloria, Gloria in excelsis Gloria' under the stars on a frosty night. Ian McMaster, then consul in Florence and a Governor, said of Downe that he felt it had a vaguely Florentine atmosphere: civilised, art-loving, beautiful. Yes indeed. Et in Arcadia ego.

M E Batstone (Milford, 1950)

I was the first Irish girl to arrive after the war, and I travelled to Downe by boat and two trains. It took all night, and the accents at Euston baffled me when I tried to procure a taxi with my trunk, my hand luggage, and a lacrosse stick. Eventually I got the 'scrum' from Paddington. The school seemed vast but the grounds and surrounding countryside were beautiful. Unlike in Ireland, where we celebrated Halloween the night before All Saints Day, November 1st, we had to observe Guy Fawkes and Bonfire Night on November 5th. The best place to see the county of Berkshire's hilltops alight was the Chapel Tower which gave a 360 degree view. Timed to perfection, we slipped into the belfry as the Senior who had been ringing the bell came out. Then we sang Evensong above the Chapel roof, and ran back to the Dining Room to our places for tea like little angels.

Alison Carter (Budd, 1952)

Miss Henriques was Head of Art and gave us such encouragement. She organised the Sketch Club and one outing was the time I remember at Downe above all others, a moment of total happiness. We sat by the riverbank at Streatley and spent a glorious day drawing and painting the bridge. At the moment of mixing watercolours in my metal paint box brought from home I felt I knew what my schooling was all about: it had kindled my love of music, drama, and art, enhanced the joy of love of nature, and the result was I felt I could do absolutely anything I put my mind to.

As the youngest admiral in the Royal Navy my father expected a longer career, but contrary to these hopes he was retired while I was in the Fifth Form, which led to the abrupt end of my education. Shortly after we had sat our General Certificate exams the moment came when it was the last day of school. Bereft, I gazed back out of the bus to see our teachers and the school buildings vanish away. My sanctuary was gone. Within weeks my father was killed and it was Miss Medley who promptly came to the rescue. She saw to it that, free of charge, I returned to live at school for a few weeks in Michaelmas. She showed such compassion and counselled well, if starkly. I had hoped to go to Art School in Florence, but this was now not an option in my penniless state. Straight from the shoulder she said, 'Everything is now up to you. Only you can make a success of your life . . . or you can fail completely. You must choose for yourself.' Within two years I'd become a self-taught advertising copywriter in New York, then a fashion journalist in Fleet Street, and later, when a single parent, raised a family solely on the strength of my pen.

Years later, at a DHSA meeting, the discussion turned to why in our time at Downe – the early 1930s to the late 1950s – none of us on the whole had rebelled. 'There was no need,' said an eighty-year-old, 'because we were each treated as an individual regardless of our age. Consequently everything felt normal.'

Elizabeth Dickson (1952)

Hair washing

All those who were at the school up to the 1960s remember the ritual of hair washing. This was only allowed once a fortnight, unless you were a particular 'greasy'. There were no hair dryers, so the girls went outside to brush their hair dry in the wind and would then wear a bright green woollen headscarf for the rest of the day. In winter they were sometimes allowed to dry their hair by the blazing log fire in the Drawing Room. Joan Jerrett (Wernham, 1960) recalls that, 'Having gone though all this rigmarole, we used to return to our house, wet our hair again, and set it in rollers! We then sat through the afternoon lessons in rollers and headscarves, dashing to our rooms just before evening Chapel to remove them.'

opened a year later. Old Seniors' Weekend in June 1957 was an occasion to remember, as Miss Medley recorded in the *Magazine*: 'It was the family feeling that was so evident on June 22nd of this year. Old Seniors came in their hundreds to show their affection for Miss Willis and to visit, not so much their old school, as a place that had once been their home. Mothers and daughters together were the rule rather than the exception, sharing the same memories and often the same jokes, and as for diversity – there were old and young, of course, that goes without saying; but there were also every kind of vocation, profession, career, occupation, employment, and plain job represented. Had, on that Saturday afternoon in June, some cataclysm overtaken the rest of the world and left us untouched, we could have started a new world, with law-makers, educationalists, writers, musicians, artists, doctors, nurses, teachers, cooks, and so on, and even a second generation (for many husbands had been impelled by curiosity to come to see why their wives were so delightful and

The Coronation frieze
in 1953 and the Jubilee
frieze, by Caroline
Horsbrugh, in 1957

66 **Swimming in the outdoor pool in the 1970s**

The Moore and Bradley-Moore families have had a long and fruitful association with Downe House. In the early days when Downe House was still in Kent and the school was new and small, Alice Moore, my aunt, was among the early pupils. Her father had died when his children were young and in 1908 Miss Willis had taken her in with her mother, as they were old friends of the family. My father Ralph, Alice's brother, also spent his holidays there. Alice Moore became a professional musician and returned to the school to teach music.

My father spent many years abroad but returned to England with his wife and family in 1944. They had very little money and no jobs, but Miss Willis – or Aunt Olive, as we called her – came to the rescue by finding accommodation for the family in Cold Ash, helping my mother, who was a doctor, to find a job in general practice in Thatcham, and accepting me into the school much younger than usual. I was a day girl for two years as we lived just outside the school gates, and then I became a boarder. My mother was appointed to Downe House as school doctor, a role she fulfilled for many years.

Alice Greenwood (Bradley-Moore, 1953)

attractive!), and we like to think that it would indeed have been a "brave new world".'

As the 1958 *Magazine* records, Jubilee Hall was opened on June 15th 1958: 'As car after car turned into the drive, one felt that someone had made a mistake somewhere and Seniors' Weekend had arrived early. But this was the first concert in Jubilee Hall, given by Dame Myra Hess on her own piano, with Orchestra, Choral, and many Old Seniors and friends of the school. . . . Unbelievably, it was a beautiful day, June at its most flaming, and made hotter by excitement. . . . And now that it is behind us, we look back with gratitude for the hard work and planning of so many people, for Dame Myra's friendship, and for the musical tradition of the school. We look forward, too, to listening to the record of the concert itself; and, further ahead, to hearing all the "sounds and sweet airs" that will be heard in the Hall in the

In 1950, after I had suffered several years at a small repressive boarding school, my parents sent me to Downe. I went with a heavy heart, expecting more of the same on a larger scale. The uniform sounded strange: a djibbah? topped by a cloak? I resigned myself to a future of challenging mysteries. Soon after arriving I ventured some important questions to my colleagues:

Are we allowed to climb trees?

Of course!

Where are the bounds?

The what?

Well, where can't we go?

We're not allowed to cross the Bath Road but otherwise everywhere.

WHAT?

Yes, as long as we ask Miss Medley and go in threes.

Gradually the ethos of this extraordinary school became clear. Rules were few, but fair and sensible. We were expected to take responsibility for our actions and accept the consequences if we didn't. It all made total sense.

Alison Burgess (Cummings, 1954)

I was a constant pain to Miss Medley (my father was a distant cousin – it was very trying!). I wrote an article on the coronation, relating my amazing day in the pouring rain in London among the patriotic crowds. To my horror this was included in the school magazine that year. Miss Medley was not pleased when I admitted to her that I had made it up and watched the whole thing on television. Another time I had been in a shooting match against Bradfield where I had a cousin. He saw the results on their notice-board the following day and thought that he and a few friends would cycle over and see us. On arrival he asked to see Miss Medley. What a mistake! She was not amused, and didn't tell me they'd been over until much later that term.

Carolyn Taylor (Medley, 1955)

As I lived on the Isle of Man, getting to Newbury and back was a huge solo adventure – I always did this on my own from the age of twelve. It required me to leave on the 9am boat to Liverpool which took four hours, and then – with the invaluable help of porters, train guards, and taxis – getting the train to Euston, crossing London to Paddington, and then changing at Datchet. I eventually arrived at Newbury at 8pm. Mr Pocock, the school driver, always met me and on my arrival at school Sister Kite would give me a warm welcome and a hot chocolate.

Deirdre Green (Cain, 1956)

I arrived at Downe on a cold winter morning in January 1952 aged eleven years and eleven months – the second youngest girl in the school – from a warm and comfortable life in Argentina. What a culture shock! First I had to get used to being called 'Baby Brundell', which I hated but it was the tradition (my sister, five years older, was nearing the end of her Downe career). Luckily the name disappeared with my sister when she left. Next the food – I had to get used to eating such things as 'hedgehog', 'spotted dog', custard with 'blanket', and other delicacies.

Then there was the Downe jargon which was extensive and an essential part of fitting in. Some entries from my old diaries tell the story: 'went to temps', 'not a very long jaw', 'did field', 'wandered at supper', queue for the jane', 'played crosse', 'played on the gianty', 'left on a scrum bus'. All my generation will understand the meaning of these expressions!

The teaching staff were all spinsters – not a wedding ring to be seen. Most of them had nicknames, and one had to be careful not to use them to their faces. 'The Med', of course, was our venerable Headmistress, Miss Medley, who appeared to tower over the tallest girl and whose smile could turn water to ice. Then there were the Demi, the Bun, Shap, Tass, Deaky, to name but a few.

Gillian Feary (Brundell, 1956)

Drama

Like music, drama was an integral part of life at Downe House from the earliest days. The school magazines over the whole hundred years are full of accounts of school plays, house plays, dramatic entertainments, collaborations (in later years) with boys' schools, staff pantomimes, and endless occasions of enjoyment, amusement, serious hard work, and fun.

Mary Midgley (Scrutton, 1937) recalls in her memoir, *The Owl of Minerva*: 'The only kind of verse that I have ever written much of is squibs – Christmas pantomimes, staff plays, sudden spoof shows usually written in collaboration and put on at top speed. A great deal of this kind of thing went on at Downe. I was found to be able to write what was needed at amazing speed and also to suggest handy dodges for stage effects. I love this occupation, both the writing itself and the hasty improvising of properties – masks, curtains, costume changes, noises – and while as an actual actor I may not be outstanding, as a stage manager and deviser of effects at the last moment – for instance in making a pack

Shakespeare in the Cloisters

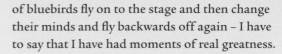

of bluebirds fly on to the stage and then change their minds and fly backwards off again – I have to say that I have had moments of real greatness.

'Drama also played a large part in my life during my last years at school when my friends and I developed an occupation called Sunday Night. This largely grew out of an overdose of Corneille, Racine, and Cyrano de Bergerac in our French lessons. On one occasion, after Sunday supper, four or five of us were gloomily wandering about the place, brooding on the Monday to come, and we just happened to be crossing the stage in the gym. Suddenly somebody – I think it was Jacobine – swung round, waved an arresting arm, and cried, "My lord, we are betrayed! The castle is besieged!" "Gadzooks, can such things be?" shouted the respondent, probably Pandora. "Oh rage, oh despair! Call in the Guards! Where is my dastard uncle?" or the like, and things went on from there. We found that we could generate a melodrama from scratch without the slightest effort. We did it enthusiastically every week, and after a time it developed into a most satisfactory soap opera. The whole thing greatly improved our approach to Monday mornings.'

Janet Wyld (Davies, 1936) remains grateful for the self-confidence she gained from being involved with drama at Downe. 'I was a shy, quiet child, but on the stage I could slide into the character I was acting and my inhibitions melted away. Under the coaching of Pam Kielly I had two excellent parts in the summer plays of my final two years: the Lady in Milton's *Comus* and Miranda in *The Tempest*.'

Josephine Walker (Holmes, 1963) was an enthusiastic actress: '*Twelfth Night* was in 1961 and I think that *As You Like It* was a couple of years earlier. I wore an unbecoming beard and ruff as Orsino in *Twelfth Night* and I can still remember the smell of the glue for the beard, and the scratchiness on one's face. My final acting triumph was in *The Importance of Being Earnest*, for which I got my acting colours (in 1962, I think). I can only remember that we laughed so much during rehearsals that Miss Barnsley – 'the Barn' – had to get quite tetchy with us.'

As with other areas of school life, drama in its many forms has evolved with the years and continues to play an important role. The last thirty years have seen many productions from a succession of talented drama staff: to be able to take part in or watch performances such as *Dancing at Lughnasa* one term and *The Doll's House* another, with *A Midsummer Night's Dream*, *The Bacchae*, and *Arcadia* interleaved with musicals such as *The King and I*, *My Fair Lady*, *Anything Goes*, and *The Sound of Music* during one's school career is a truly educative experience.

Since the early 1990s, theatre studies, later drama, has been an option for A-level and this, together with House Drama productions, has given many girls both the opportunity to act and to become experienced in the more technical aspects of directing, producing, lighting, sound systems, and stage management. While a few girls (including Geraldine James, Caroline Blakiston, Paula Bacon, Virginia Hatton, Flora Montgomery, and Georgina Rylance) have gone on to become professional actors, many more have gained enjoyment and confidence from the dramatic opportunities available.

Why, above, and *Guys and Dolls*, below

The School train – 'the scrum' – at Newbury Station in 1940

We did not question the eccentricities of the organisation, but in retrospect where else would anybody have spent endless hours polishing threepenny bits? Had their temperatures taken every day for the first three weeks of term and every weekend? Who still has 'bunny ball' rice? I once read a recipe in which this appeared and knew the author had to have been to Downe. The fact that we shared rooms and meals with people of all ages, and with the staff, means that we can converse with anyone, anywhere – I hope we learned to listen too. Moving round the Dining Room meant that you could end up, if on the High on a Friday, having to debone the Med's kipper. She feigned incompetence – but a lifetime skill was acquired.

Over forty years and many lifetimes ago, I married the man who was brave enough to see me off on the scrum from Paddington Station. It was for him (he collected signs for his study), on my last day at Downe, that I unscrewed the enamel sign in Top East that said 'pull gently – let go'. To this day I feel guilty.

Judith Horner (Nesbitt, 1956)

future, now that its life has begun.' There is an appended note: 'Gramophone records (12in LP double-sided) of this concert are being sold in aid of the Jubilee Hall Fund for 30/- each.'

Just over four years after this triumph, the opening months of 1963 saw the beginning of fundamental changes for Downe House when Nancy Medley was diagnosed with terminal cancer and took immediate retirement. In the 1962 *Magazine*, Miss Medley had noted her satisfaction that she had 'at last succeeded in appointing a Deputy Headmistress.' This was Constance Pyke, who had taught Classics at Downe from 1946 to 1953 and had rejoined the school at the beginning of the Michaelmas term in 1962. Miss Pyke soon

The whole Downe experience is so vast that it is hard to know where to begin, so I thought a few reminiscences of how it was for a new girl would be a way in. I was so happy there, because it was a place where you were allowed to be, and there was very little regimentation. The form was our unit, because houses were only where we slept, and from term to term might be changed. Our bedrooms were shared with girls from different years, and by the end of my first term I knew everybody in the school. During the first year or so, girls might be moved from one form to another, as we arrived at different ages and the strengths and weaknesses apparent in the Common Entrance papers might not be a complete picture. The odd new girl would appear, possibly from overseas, and would be absorbed, but on the whole after a year the form was usually a fairly complete unit and we saw ourselves as such.

There were various customs and traditions inculcated into us new girls. You never walked across the Loggia. You never walked along the terrace immediately outside the staff room. You kept away from the Garden Room, apart from the New Girls' party, unless summoned there. It was taboo to do up the buttons on your cloak unless you were a Senior – you had to learn the art of keeping it on your shoulders without that help.

Rosanne Adam (Watson, 1958)

I remember most about our free time: borrowing the tin trays from the Dining Room for sledging when it had snowed, or sometimes skating on Hermitage Pond; being sent off for days out with a picnic, when we would cycle to Pangbourne and hire a boat to go for a trip on the river; knitting, making birthday and Christmas cards, and creating our own packs of cards so that we could play patience or whist; pottering about the woods, digging up our hidden stores of condensed milk and licking the stuff off our palms. . . .

Patricia Jones (Strong, 1958)

I was part of a 'Gang of Eight', and our most daring escapade was a trip to Reading on the bus – out of bounds! We got hold of a bus timetable, cycled like mad to where we could pick up a bus, went up on the top deck, and began to plaster ourselves with make-up. There was a scare when we got off the bus at Reading as we saw one of our teachers, but luckily she didn't see us. We went to record shops, found a little greasy spoon café for lunch in a back street, and went to the cinema. But we could only see half the film as we had to head back to the bus stop. We took our make-up off, got our bikes, and felt we could burst with excitement and a sense of achievement!

Rosey Woodbridge (Handley, 1960)

My mother went to Downe, my three aunts went to Downe, my three sisters went to Downe, and two of my cousins went to Downe. As a result, my djibbah was so thin that you could just about see through it. My mother had founded the Growlers Society and therefore presumed that her four daughters would be tone deaf, so we didn't have individual music lessons and had HC – for Housecraft – marked on our timetables. This meant that you cleaned the dormitories or, worse, the bathrooms and loos. One way out of this was to persuade your parents to let you learn Italian, and this I did, with Mlle Tasartey, who duly arrived by train from London each week. Although the journey made her so tired that she often fell asleep during the lessons, she was a good teacher – so much so that during the O-level oral exam the examiner asked why I wasn't taking A-level.

Nicola Hulbert (Stobart, 1960)

The Giant's Stride, or gianty

'Today's Health and Safety inspectors would be horrified at this plaything,' recall the pupils who were at Downe House when this was an installation in the grounds. It consisted of a central pole with chains hung from it like a maypole, and ropes at the end of the chains. 'The whole thing rotated,' recalls Rosanne Adam (Watson, 1958), 'and the point was to run round and round it and take off using centrifugal force (a term of which we were as yet totally ignorant) and see how high and far we would fly as a result. . . . One person could do it alone, but the best flights were when several others got up enough momentum to keep it going as one jumped and helped to pull one further.' Sometimes a group of girls would hold the ropes and revolve around the pole while one of their number stayed outside them and went the other way. As the chains got tighter this girl would be swung higher and wider! Exciting stuff and great fun – but the ground underneath was covered with cinders, so barked knees and grazed elbows were the usual outcome. Juliet Rees (Gowan, 1947) recalls 'hauling some friend round and up on the Giant's Stride, or being heaved up into the air oneself. Dreadful weals on our right forearms from hanging on to the rope loop often festered, witnessing to our dedication to this thrilling (but unsupervised) activity.' Many of the Downe reminiscences mention 'the wonderful feeling of flying on the Giant's Stride'.

found herself taking over as Acting Headmistress. Miss Medley moved to a bungalow with Sister Kite, who also retired that term, but survived only until July 1963. This major loss was followed by a further great sadness in the death of Miss Willis, less than a year later in March 1964.

Many of the girls who were at Downe House at the time of Miss Medley's death remember both the desolation they felt at her illness and death and also, later, the feeling that the school was for a time without direction. 'Her absence created an irreplaceable black hole,' as Tessa Smith (Kempton, 1963) put it. And then, as Carolyn Jack (1968) recalls, 'We were the "generation of the three heads", not the best time in the hundred years – though I suppose it is special that we were the last year to know both Miss Willis and Miss Medley.'

Janet Hesketh (Laurie, 1965) is typical: 'With hindsight they truly were the wilderness years, a view that I'm sure the academic/sporting/music records will support. Nancy Medley, the only reason I had been sent to the school, died suddenly and there was a sense, even to a thirteen-year-old, of the place being rudderless. We quickly took responsibility for our own health and happiness and did an excellent job on both counts. Racing Demon world records were set, Mason's sale of frozen cakes doubled year on year, Chapel Tower was scaled, roll-ups of oak leaves were inhaled, the "Love Me Do" track wore through the vinyl, Ian Fleming's books were currency, and friendships, like no others, were cemented. I have no memories, either good or bad, of the learning process. I was steadfastly resistant to engaging my brain. I busied about in my sloppy djibbah jersey and multicoloured socks just . . . well, being busy. Missed opportunities, certainly, but a better environment in which to grow up and put down a taproot before hitting London at its height, I cannot imagine.'

These were sad years indeed for Downe House, with the loss of the two charismatic headmistresses who had steered the school through its first fifty-five years. Miss Pyke filled the gap until the beginning of the next school year, when Jennifer Bourdillon became Headmistress. The new Head records in the 1964 *Magazine* her gratitude that she had had the good fortune to meet Miss Willis before her death, and had the assurance of her goodwill. But there was not to be a long period of continuity: Mrs Bourdillon resigned at the end of the 1966 summer term with the intention of continuing in office until summer 1967, but was forced by ill health to leave at the end of the 1966 Michaelmas term. She was succeeded in January 1967 by Pamela Wilson, who had been a member of the English staff for some years.

Mrs Wilson at her retirement dinner, left, and Mrs Bourdillon, above

One vivid memory is going on the school train (steam, of course!) from Paddington with emotional stiff-upper-lip farewells to be replaced as soon as the first corner was turned by the excited exchange of holiday news with friends. In the summer the sun always seems to be shining as we shed our djibbahs for brightly coloured tunics. After Baghdad, the outdoor, freezing, greenish swimming pool was definitely a little different from what I was used to but, as it was my only team sport, I got on with it! At the time, I didn't realise how important making friends is. I'm still in contact with many. We went twice a day to Chapel. Looking back, this was lovely and proved to be a great foundation of life and faith. I was in Junior Choir and Jacqueline du Pre came to play in the newly-built Jubilee Hall. Her sister Hilary taught the flute at Downe. There were so many good things: the amazing safe space of the grounds and the teaching of English were two of them. I have clear memories of us careering around the Cloisters rehearsing for *Peter and the Wolf*. We were taught responsibility from a young age as head of a small dormitory in East or West – though we didn't call them dormitories! The Olive Willis ethos was still about: everyone was interesting and each girl was expected to appear interesting, even going as far as making the recitation of names in the telephone directory sound interesting!

Susan Main (Chaplin, 1962)

Unfortunately when I was there the Headmistress, Nancy Medley, was terminally ill so we weren't exactly kept in line academically. However, I do have warm memories of Downe, in the main because of the many eccentric rules and regulations. I'm sure the practice of the bucket coming round the dormitories twice a week to collect our underwear has long ceased: someone was given the job of calling our 'vests, socks, and linings'. Unusually, there was no smoking behind the bicycle shed. I think we were all put off by the aroma of our chain-smoking Headmistress, Deaconess, and French mistress. Much to my relief there was no competitive system, no top of the class, no gaining marks for houses. I think this encouraged a sense of good feeling towards each other, and the most important legacy for me is the enduring friendships I made at Downe.

Sophie Baker (1962)

73

74

In our first term the new girls were invited to a Sunday afternoon tea with Miss Willis at Hill House. I had hardly ever eaten scones and jam, let alone with cream too! Miss Willis was a formidable old lady then, but always still read the lesson at Seniors Weekend. 'Go to the ant, thou sluggard, consider her ways and be wise' with 'ant' pronounced 'aunt', which older girls told us had once been Downe slang for the lavatory, as 'jane' was in our time.

Ann Budd (Lawson, 1964)

I was part of a three-generation family at Downe (below): my mother, Joan Davies (Cooke, 1937); her three daughters – my sister, Susan Sinclair, who left in 1962, myself, and our younger sister, Alison Day, who left in 1969. My two daughters, Tessa and Zaria, left in 1994 and 1999, and Susie's daughter, Helen, left in 2002.

I recently came across several letters I wrote home, which eloquently bring back the time I spent at Downe. One records the journey back from Miss Willis's memorial service in London: 'Our bus broke down just outside Thatcham. The diesel engine conked out so the steering followed suit. We nearly made our way into the nearest pub but the rescue bus arrived just in time. Maddening!' There are other memories of 'flu jabs with separate syringes for each person thus contradicting rumours about blunt needles' and a dance with boys from all the local schools which was stopped early because some of the boys got bored and started to wander round outside Jubilee Hall.

Cynthia Rich (Davies, 1964)

Electronics in the 1980s

Mrs Bourdillon's lasting legacy was the new Science Block, opened in October 1967 by Professor Dorothy Hodgkin, with Dame Rosemary Murray, Old Senior and Chairman of the Governors, in attendance. This increased support for science was part of a growing number of changes, including the retirement of many of the stalwarts of the school's earlier history. Yet during these years the organisation, structure, and ethos of the school remained much as it had been for the whole of its history, conforming to Miss Willis's views on integration, pastoral care, and freedom. Mrs Wilson had a commanding presence and a deep reverence for the values and traditions that she had inherited. But the world – and the world of education – was moving on, and towards the end of her tenure she was beginning to realise that changes would have to be made. Her editorial in the *Magazine* for 1976–77 expresses her thinking on these issues:

10 EVENING POST Monday, October 9, 1967

Nobel prizewinner opens Berks school science lab

PROFESSOR Dorothy Hodgkin, Nobel chemistry prize winner, opened the £30,000 science laboratory at Downe House, the girl's public school at Hermitage, on Saturday.

The attractive single-storey building is a Swiss design and has four spacious laboratories for physics, chemistry and biology plus a preparation room and staff room.

Half the cost of the

From Peter Kimber, Newbury

laboratory is being met by the Olive Willis Memorial Fund — named after the school's founder.

Professor Hodgkin said: "We need more women scientists. In my day there were very few — today there are many more but we still need more. With this new laboratory, I hope many girls will take up scientific subjects."

Professor Hodgkin discovered vitamin V 12. She was elected a Fellow of the Royal Society in 1947 and was awarded the Society's gold medal in 1956.

In 1964 she was awarded the Nobel prize for chemistry — which only two other women have won.

Professor Hodgkin, pictured above right, looks over the new lab with Dr. Rosemary Murray, chairman of Downe House Board of Governors.

'Miss Willis felt that girls did not respond as happily as their brothers to a conventional house system and the individual at Downe House has always been accorded the opportunity to change her sleeping arrangements from term to term, regardless of age or seniority. This tried and excellent practice, however, depends upon extensive

75

One elderly lady on the school scene was Crift, as we called her, her real name being Miss Croft. She was a friend of Miss Medley and seemed to have no particular job. She tended various bits of garden and appeared in surprising places at unexpected moments. Crift was always kind and never minded if we broke the rules. We used to tell her all sorts of secrets. She was an antidote to some of the other more Dickensian characters on the staff – and, unlike many of my contemporaries, who were terrified of her, I greatly admired Miss Medley. Tall, emaciated, stooped, constantly smoking, always dressed in grey, she was an alarming and wraith-like figure; but to me, as a shy academic child, she was extremely kind and encouraging.

That was Downe when I arrived in 1961; by 1966 it had loosened up considerably. We had brilliant history and English teachers in the form of Miss Smith and Miss Gosse. Although it was fashionable to say that you never learnt a thing, there was superb teaching there if you wanted it. However, it was extraordinarily difficult to work as much as one would have liked to: I got into great trouble for revising in the Drying Room (next to Bottom South) at night, being condemned to eat breakfast on the 'Little High' all on my own for a week. This seems a surprising way to treat a willing swot of fourteen!

Rosemary Andreae (Gilbert, 1966)

In January 1962 I arrived in Remove C, rising twelve years old. Every desk had an incredibly stiff green canvas bag with two leather handles hanging on a hook at the side. This was for carrying books from one lesson to another, but they were never used by anybody, as the fashion was for running along with your folders and books cradled in your arms, tucked under your bust if you had one. Friday evening: collecting sixpence pocket money from Miss Young up in the room above Miss Medley's study. Here we also played billiards, and had to try to remember not to let the cue drop vertically when we wanted to take our shot, as it thumped on the ceiling of the Med's study and she might appear up her stairs very silently, like an apparition, to ask you to stop.

Caroline Perkins (McCutcheon, 1967)

supervision, often at unsocial hours, and in 1977 it presents difficulties for the few resident staff. . . . We plan, now, to reorganise the school community into five groups: two Junior, two Middle, and one Senior, placing each group in the charge of a non-teaching Housemistress [or matron] and a House Tutor. The latter will watch personally over the academic progress and general welfare of each girl in her charge for two years, after which the promotion of the child to a different tutelage, and another House, will automatically follow. The House Tutor will provide easy access to parents and to pupils alike, and will maintain close relations with teaching and administrative staff. The

In October 1962 (I was twelve) John F Kennedy announced that he had received intelligence about the installation of Soviet missiles in Cuba. It started two weeks of tension between the Kremlin and the White House as the US imposed a naval blockade of Cuba and demanded the removal of the missiles. All over the world people were terrified, thinking a nuclear war was imminent. It filtered through to us at Downe, and I remember spending a fearful week worrying with my friends about something I didn't quite understand, wishing I was at home with my family, and saying tearful goodbyes on the netball court. We truly believed that this was the end of the world as we knew it and that the Third World War was upon us.

Juliet Harkness (Wilson, 1968)

The orchestra accompanying *School for Scandal* in 1969

76

I arrived at Downe in January 1962 when I was eleven. It was a dark and forbidding place full of tall pine trees and dank passageways, and pretty alarming whatever the time of year. My first room was in Top West and the scary Miss Samuels (Latin) was our Housemistress. I shared with two other girls who bullied me and called me common because my name was Thomas and everyone else seemed to have double-barrelled names and to own half of Warwickshire.

And then there was Miss Medley – tall and thin with a scraped-back bun of steely grey, and a long narrow suit to match. She used to prowl the corridors at night to make sure no-one was talking after lights. You could never hear her coming, but you could smell her; cigarette smoke – her eventual downfall – hung around her in a great fog and only added to her sense of menace. The Med, as we called her, used to tell ghost stories to the Remove up in the Drawing Room – really scary stories that then got handed down through the school. She told them in the present tense as if they were happening now, and she had a very deep, compelling voice that was quiet but powerful and extremely frightening. The school ghost was called Arabella. I can't remember what was supposed to have happened to her, but she was said to walk across the gallery above the gym and then throw herself off – but only at midnight on Halloween. That was an extremely busy time for all of us: if you looked into the mirror at the end of South Way above the Dining Room at midnight on Halloween, you would see your future husband standing behind you with a knife – but if you turned round to look at him he would stab you! And if you ran round the High three times, again on the dot of midnight, you would bump into your future husband coming the other way.

Anything to do with Boys was severely frowned upon. I was almost expelled, twice, for that reason. Once it was for receiving a telegram from a boyfriend arranging a meeting which, because it was a telegram, was opened and shown to the Headmistress, Constance Pyke. She went out to meet him instead, and didn't tell me about it till next day, when she told me I had gone too far and that she had rung my father and told him to come and take me away. The second time was on a Sunday night at Ancren Gate

when a boy I knew had to drive me back to school as my mother was too ill, and I was caught giving him cocoa in my bedroom. That didn't go down at all well, but again my father refused to have me at home so the school had to keep me. When Pamela Wilson became Head, she thought the only way to deal with me was to make me Head Senior!

Life at Downe was terrifying, intimidating, overwhelming; it was also inspiring, thrilling, challenging, and rewarding – and the place where I formed lifelong friendships, including one with the theatre.

Geraldine James (Thomas, 1968)

78

Chapel was compulsory twice a day every day, and missing a service was hard to do. After the school had filed in, the Seniors would do a check round classrooms, music room, houses, and grounds. But I have a clear memory of successfully missing Evensong one winter evening. Three of us hid under our metal beds in Middle South, clinging tightly to the underside of the beds, fingers pinched by the bedsprings as the Seniors made their way through the house, opening and shutting bedroom doors. We hardly dared to breathe as we suffered feelings of both excitement and dread and were trying to suppress uncontrollable giggles. And we were not caught!

Geri Rider (Woodrow, 1969)

Downe was different from other girls' boarding schools and we were proud of it. It was idiosyncratic. The vertical integration for meals and the mixed ages in the 'rooms' (never say 'dormitory') were exceptional for building a wide range of friendships. There was the established hierarchy of the most junior person in the room having the bed behind the door. Also you were expected to have a 'pash' (never say 'crush') on someone in the Sixth Form. We did not go to the loo or the bog, and would certainly never go to the toilet, but to the 'jane'. The academic results, especially in science subjects, were not a strength during my time. Downe excelled in being eccentrically pragmatic. Where else would you be encouraged to play a musical instrument by the implementation of 'Housecraft' – cleaning the dormitories, sorry rooms – as the penalty for not doing so? Where else would you not be allowed on school trips wearing the school uniform? It was comfortable but unattractive and was often recycled for generations – in other words, it was tatty. Downe House celebrated and developed the individual and offered an environment within which lifelong friendships could form. My time at Downe produced more gain than pain, and my life is richer for my experiences there and the friendships made.

Rosie Leggo (Bunting, 1970)

Not the best of times for Downe, I think; somewhat unstable – Mrs Bourdillon was Headmistress when we arrived, then Mrs Wilson. At a reunion gathering a few years ago there were several of my contemporaries who were quite angry (*sic*) at what they felt had been an inadequate education. But there were brighter spots. The Literary Society ('Lit') used to meet in Miss Gosse's bungalow on Saturdays. She had a terrier called Sirius. I also remember her leaving out a doodled drawing of a spirited horse to remind herself that the 'charger' for the lawnmower was on!

When the alarm for fire practice sounded you had to go to the Concert Room where you collected a wooden 'tally' marked with your room number and assembled together with the rest of your 'house' for your Housemistress to make a roll call. If anyone was missing it would be immediately apparent as the corresponding tally would still be on its labelled hook (they were hung all round the walls).

Mary Murphy (Pierce, 1970)

The Concert Room
now and in 1935

motivating principles of the original foundation can be maintained and, far from acting against the theories of our Founder, we are now tailoring them to meet the needs of today. It is 100 years now since she was born, on October 26th 1877, and this seems an appropriate moment to make a change in part of the school's structure.'

A year later Mrs Wilson retired, 'with a deep sense of thankfulness for the sixteen years I have spent here as teacher and Headmistress.' Her final message to the school reiterated her belief that, despite the fact that 'the world she knew has changed, and standards in education are now less predictable . . . the beliefs of Olive Willis remain inviolate. I have, throughout, been conscious of a special kind of atmosphere comprising warmth, endeavour, and a love which embraces the whole community – everyone connected with the school.

I have only happy memories of Downe House. We were always terribly naughty and pushed every boundary to the limits. We had so many shared adventures and formed lifelong friendships. I remember the practice cells where we would shove the piano forward and squeeze in behind to see if we could sit through someone's lesson without being discovered – equal agony for the pupil whose lesson it was as well as the hidden friend! Punishments from the Seniors usually took the form of wood detention, when we had to fill a huge wicker basket with kindling for their fire. Or we were made to stand on a table in front of the whole Upper Sixth and sing a hymn. We would always sing the longest hymn we knew, as out of tune as possible, and pretend not to be at all scared or humiliated.

Julia Bannister (Talbot-Rice, 1974)

My parents were posted with Shell to Tokyo, so along with my two sisters we flew in each term. There were very few of us from abroad, and we were known as the 'aeroplane children'. I remember my very first arrival: Mrs Wilson stood framed in the vestibule door as Mr Pocock drove us in at some late hour after a twenty-hour flight to Heathrow. 'Ah!' she beamed. 'So the Hill sisters have all arrived at last.' I relied heavily on the generosity of my Downe friends to take me into their homes at exeats. In all the years I was there I never had to spend those times at school. Downe engendered a real family closeness and warmth which reflected itself in the great friendship and generosity of spirit I saw and needed as I visited and stayed with so many Downe girls' families. It was precisely at those times that homesickness would otherwise have struck hardest.

Gillian Lee (Hill, 1975)

80

My mother, Sally Woodhouse (Haggard, 1951), was at Downe, and one of my father's rather over-used remarks about Downe House girls was that if you happened to be a husband of one, you'd be lucky if you were not deaf by the age of forty! While I was at the school, one Sunday afternoon Mrs Wilson asked me to play tennis with her son, Tig. While I was waiting nervously in the Drawing Room for my opponent to appear, I happened to remark that I had lost a button on the waistband of my tennis skirt. The next thing was seeing Mrs Wilson pulling up her skirt – a rather well-fitting, tweed, A-line number – and fishing out a baby's nappy pin from her pink-edged corset to help me with my problem. I looked at her with different eyes from then on.

Joanna Morris (Woodhouse, 1975)

Our English teacher, Mrs Dawson, featured in a drama that occurred on the Mayday Bank Holiday, which the school did not observe. It was put about that it would be terrific fun if we all went on strike about this, so after Chapel everyone started shouting and chanting and refusing to go to their classrooms. Mrs Dawson marched towards a group of us, tears of rage in her eyes, and hoarsely declared: 'If you go on strike now, I will go on strike when it's time for your O-levels.' This was brilliantly effective, and of course we all backed down – aided by the weather as it had started to rain! My parents later removed me from the school in the belief that it had had the wrong sort of influence on me. But after my sheltered upbringing, Downe House forced me into becoming a great deal more independent. I recall it as a shocking, toughening-up process, the main rewards being the extremely close friendships that were made, solid barriers against pain.

Vivien Tucker (Forestier-Walker, 1976)

I am certain that Downe is for ever imbued with the spirit of its Founder and this, despite reforms, rebuilding, and reorganisation, is indestructible. The heritage lives on.'

But equally, there was now urgent need for development and change and the new Headmistress, who took up office at the beginning of the 1978/9 school year, was appointed precisely in order to take this challenge on. Suzanne Farr was to make an immediate and lasting impression on the school.

I think the title of this book is so apt, because it suggests rather beautifully the school's hidden depths. In this regard, I wonder how the book will encompass the 'downs' as well as the 'ups'. Marvellous and wonderful and jolly lacrosse sticks? Or recognition that at times there were failures too? My first memories of my time at Downe are definitely more 'Northanger Abbey' than 'Mansfield Park'. In my dreams I still wander down dark gloomy corridors and stone staircases cut into the hillside to the echoing sound of dripping water as ice melts from leaking roofs and collapsed gutters! No wonder I jibbed in my djibbah if I had to go alone to retrieve a textbook during evening prep.

Then the new broom came and swept the cobwebs away, very gradually of course – carpets on the floors, lined curtains, young enthusiastic teachers, an indoor swimming pool, and boys to dinner. The myths and ghosts, what happened to them? If you listen carefully, are they still whispering among the Cloisters?

Rose Persson (Colman, 1977)

Music

Throughout the entire first hundred years Downe House has been renowned for its music. Inspirational teachers, highly gifted pupils, top-class visiting musicians, and excellent facilities have combined to ensure that music has always been at the centre of life at Downe.

It started early. Marjorie Gunn became a part of Downe House music and drama very soon after the school opened, visiting to give concerts and take part in plays. She gave up a promising solo career in favour of teaching, which she felt to be her true vocation, and was – to quote Anne Ridler – 'one of those rare teachers in whom the sap of enthusiasm seems inexhaustible. Each of her pupils, even the veriest beginner, felt herself unique, and potentially a musician. The high standards which she retained, and the full musical life which she combined with her teaching life, helped to raise Downe's achievement above the common level reached in those days.'

Miss Gunn

Summer Music School advertisement, 1954

present pupils as well as some fathers and husbands. It was a memorable occasion.

An early initiative in teaching composition at the school was due to the presence on the staff of Robin Milford, Olive Willis's godson, whose gentle but effective teaching enabled the girls to give several concerts of their own compositions. His own compositions were often given their first performance at Downe House, and he also wrote most of the music for the plays and dance-dramas performed during those years. One of his songs, a setting of Robert Bridges' 'I love all beauteous things', became a staple item in Choral's repertoire.

Marjorie Gunn was a great friend of Dame Myra Hess, who maintained a lively interest in the school and several times came to play, usually bringing her own piano. Twice, the orchestra had the thrilling experience of playing the Bach D Minor Piano Concerto with her as soloist. Rosamund Peirson (Hoare, 1952) was the orchestra leader on one of those occasions, in 1951: 'Never before, and rarely since, have I experienced such electrifying power as came from Dame Myra's personality in the performance, which caught us all up and seemed to lift us to a new level. I can still hear in my mind the brilliance of the sounds as she brought the piano alive, and the sound of her voice as she encouraged us at

She was soon joined at the school by Dorothy Read ('the Demi'), who began to teach piano and singing, bringing her own special gifts to the task: her energy, and her never failing interest in exploring new music and fresh techniques. These two teachers inspired a remarkable fifty years of music-making at Downe, and a tradition of excellence which has persisted. Indeed, Miss Gunn's fiftieth anniversary at the school was celebrated in 1964 with a splendid concert in Jubilee Hall, with music provided by past and

Looking from the grounds over the Berkshire Downs
The covered cloisters give access to the music studios and practice rooms

SUMMER HOLIDAY MUSIC MAKING

At DOWNE HOUSE, BERKS
Three Residential Courses from 29th July
£7 . 17 . 6 per week inclusive

Although these Courses are attended by experienced musicians, provision is made for those of moderate attainments. Private Lessons may be arranged.

Write for the complete programme which gives the list of exceptionally interesting music to be rehearsed and performed

CHAMBER MUSIC WEEK
beginning 29th July under the direction of
IVOR JAMES, C.B.E., F.R.C.M., Hon.R.A.M.
Chamber Music Groups will be coached in works of their own choice from the Syllabus. There will be a Chamber Ensemble Class. The MENGES QUARTET will give a Concert each evening.

ORCHESTRAL WEEK
beginning 5th August under the direction of
EDRIC CUNDELL, C.B.E., Hon.R.A.M., F.G.S.M.
Orchestral playing in rehearsal and performance ; Sectional tuition by experienced Coaches ; Ensemble Groups.
Conductors : EDRIC CUNDELL, NORMAN DEL MAR, ALEXANDER GIBSON.

CHORAL WEEK
A SPECIAL WEEK FOR SINGERS
beginning 12th August under the direction of
DR. REGINALD JACQUES
Motets and Madrigals .. .. .. BORIS ORD, M.A., B.Mus.
Course for Conductors .. .. DR. REGINALD JACQUES
The Art of Singing .. .. .. SIR STEUART WILSON
Accompanists' & Music-Makers' Course DR. THORNTON LOFTHOUSE
String Orchestra .. .. .. DR. REGINALD JACQUES
Accompanist .. .. HUBERT DAWKES, B.Mus.

Massed Choral Singing

RECORDER WEEK
beginning 5th August under the direction of
EDGAR HUNT, L.R.A.M., F.T.C.L.
assisted by ROBERT SALKELD, A.R.C.M.
Instruction and practice in ensemble playing. Tuition for beginners

The FEDERATION of FESTIVALS, 106 Gloucester Place, London, W.1

rehearsal.' Most of the memories of Downe House at this time include enthusiastic reminiscences of Dame Myra's visits, and she was later to play at the opening of Jubilee Hall in 1958.

Katharine McCulloch (Inglis, 1925) played both the piano and the violin while she was at the school: 'Marjorie Gunn was a very good teacher and rather a wild type. Her sister, Sazzie, taught the cello and the two of them got a small orchestra going. One day when we were at choir practice the violin teacher came in and said "I know you all play the piano and a second instrument, except you (pointing to one girl). Would you like to learn to play the oboe as we need one in the orchestra?" The girl, Evelyn Rothwell, said she would, and kept it up in a big way after she left school, playing and teaching, and eventually became one of the leading oboists in the country and married John Barbirolli, the well-known conductor.'

Diana Richmond (Galbraith, 1931) writes lyrically about music at Downe: 'My unique, special regard is reserved for Miss Read who strikes me, I believe, as the best teacher I ever studied with. I can see her now, confident, cheerful, standing upright as though permanently just about to brim into song, rallying any pupil, choir, or class with her loving enthusiasm. She taught me the piano, and she believed I could do much more than I ever achieved. But all one term my work in those jingling little practice cells was abandoned one day a week because Evelyn Rothwell was playing her oboe next door and I preferred to listen.'

Rosemary Powell (James, 1932) recalls that in the late 1920s the Downe House orchestra, under Miss Gunn, almost invariably won schools competitions. One year they even beat St Paul's whose orchestra was conducted by Holst in a composition he had written specially for them. After that, Downe was asked not to enter future competitions as other schools were withdrawing, saying that they had no chance! Elizabeth Adams (Acland, 1946) remembers 'Amaryllis Fleming, who became one of the leading cellists of the mid-twentieth century and was a sixth-former at Downe in the early 1940s. Her obituary in *The Times*, after her death in late July 1999 at the age of 73, described her time at Downe as ". . . some stormy years, locked in combat with authority", but she was nevertheless one of the brightest stars the school ever produced.'

M E Batstone (Milford, 1950) was Marjorie Gunn's god-daughter and now owns the brooch presented to Miss Gunn on the occasion of her fortieth anniversary at the school in 1954. It is in the form of a sheaf of corn because, as Miss Willis said, 'you come bringing your sheaves with you.' Among Mrs Batstone's memories of music-making at Downe is that 'Miss Willis herself so believed in the importance of music that she took up the fiddle and played, not well but valiantly, among the second violins in the orchestra for a time. Miss Read, in 1947, took much of the school to Oxford to sing, with other schools and the Oxford Bach choir, the Bach B Minor Mass, conducted by Jacques with the Jacques orchestra, and two years later to the Albert Hall with the London Bach choir; high spots indeed!'

'I was lucky enough to have a music scholarship,' recalls Eileen Field (Gower, 1965), 'and my happiest times were spent making music and attending extremely good concerts, including a cello recital given by Jacqueline du Pre when she was still a teenager. "Fizzy" Fairbank, Director of Music, spurred us on with care and strictness and I went on to make my career as a professional musician. Choral rehearsals and performances were always a thrill and I had my first opportunities to sing solos and conduct. Although I was a soprano Miss Fairbank put me with the altos "to help with sight-singing", for which I will always be grateful. Pat Alderton was also an inspiration and, among other things, took one or two of us on a memorable outing to play the organ at Eton College Chapel.'

84

Junior Choral in the Chapel

To be accepted for Choral was a great accolade, and inspires many memories. Juliet Rees (Gowan, 1947) 'soon found myself in Choral – and what amazing luck! Our choir went with "massed school choirs" to the Albert Hall, to sing Bach's B Minor Mass. Singing in Choral was, at all times and seasons, a wonder and a delight – perhaps especially so at Christmas when we trudged through the snowy fields singing to the staff houses and in between. Once a harpist came and we sang Benjamin Britten's brilliant *Ceremony of Carols* – crisp, frosty, and full of mystery. From Choral on Sundays, we used to dash like predators to Sunday lunch – the best meal of the week. The last music we sang (eg "Greetings") is forever resonant with roast lamb and roast potatoes – and greed!'

Marion Milford (1949) remembers 'going with Choral to sing carols for the Finzis' Christmas concerts, little knowing that I would sing solo for Gerald and, after his death, for his son, Christopher (Kiffer), for nearly forty years. But my most amazing memory is that I was one of the few people to take the wind out of Miss Willis's sails. About two weeks before we were due to perform *The Tempest* for the Old Seniors, I met Miss Willis and she said to me, "I'm afraid your school work is suffering and if it doesn't improve I'll have to take Ariel away from you." "OK," said I, as I knew I had only been given the part as I was evidently the only "child" considered capable of singing the songs.'

For Susan Beale (Brierley, 1954), 'Most memorable was the music-making. Singing in

Choral in Worcester Cathedral in 1987

86

Choral and every day in Chapel engendered a lifelong and continuing enjoyment, and indeed led to my meeting my husband-to-be when we were singing in the Royal Choral Society under Sir Malcolm Sargent. Miss Gunn was a huge influence, teaching violin in room 15 and conducting Orchestra in Thursday evenings, always with her little dog Trot alongside.'

Claire Meyer (1980) is grateful to this day that 'Downe House gave me the wonderful opportunity of immersing myself in my first love – music – and equally my second – art. I was so insistent on practising the piano as much as I could that I was given the Music Block key so that I could practice until ten o'clock at night. I also spent many happy hours in the piano prac cells in the Cloisters. Christmas at Downe was always special. I was honoured to be Head of Choral and enjoyed each year the tradition of wearing our cloaks and walking round the balcony in the Dining Room with candles singing carols.'

Anthea Steel (Wilson, 1957) was a pupil at Downe in the 1950s, but her fond memories of music at the school are enhanced by her later time there when she was the Assistant

Housemistress of Aisholt at the same time as her daughter, Katy, was a pupil. This came about because Anthea's husband, Christopher Steel, had to take early retirement, due to ill health, from his post as Director of Music at Bradfield. The family thereafter divided their time between

Choral with Mr Selby in the British Embassy, Washington, in 1983, above, and in France in the early 1990s, left

their flat in Aisholt and the family home in Oxfordshire, and Christopher devoted the rest of his life to composition. He wrote two pieces for the 1980s Downe musicians: one was a flute ensemble commissioned by Hilary Finzi and the other was a Christmas carol for the Junior Choir. Two of his cantatas were also performed in Chapel: 'Gethsemane' and 'Mary Magdalene', both with words by Boris Pasternak.

Not everyone at Downe was musical. Susan Schanche (Gaddum, 1947) 'was grateful to find that Downe was broad-minded as regards singing, and it was possible to qualify as a "growler" and be let off choir practice after Chapel. I entered for the "growler test" as soon as possible, and succeeded in qualifying, joining the

Les Choristes de
Downe House Choral
ensemble anglais
direction: Trevor Selby

GRAND CONCERT

choeur et orgue
- Oeuvres anciennes et modernes -

CATHÉDRALE DE CHARTRES

VENDREDI 17 juillet - 18h.30

Entrée gratuite

Choral Society with
Radley in 1984

'Students now take for granted trips abroad to faraway places, but in the early 1980s a weekend in Suffolk singing in the Cathedrals of Ely and Bury St Edmunds was considered the height of adventure! From that small beginning we went on tour to France, singing in Notre Dame, Sainte Clothilde, and Chartres as well as giving a concert in the British Embassy in Paris. Our trip to America was an ambitious project, especially as we travelled on a shoestring, using an all-American yellow school bus driven by a monk and costing us nothing apart from the gasoline used! Our lovely driver exchanged his brown habit for a tee-shirt and jeans, and we sang in churches, cathedrals, and concert halls, culminating in a short concert at the White House and a grand reception and concert at the British Embassy in Washington.

'Operas performed at the Edinburgh Fringe Festival were just as exciting, as well as being a complete headache for all the staff involved. We attracted large audiences as musical productions were rare in the Fringe programme, and rehearsing and performing in such an atmosphere added an exhilarating dimension to the school's musical life.'

Valerie Byrom-Taylor was a music teacher at the school from 1977 to 1992, and Director of Music during her final ten years there.

'Music Weekend – a development from Seniors' Weekend – is one of Downe House's splendid traditions, when a Saturday and Sunday in May are given over to music. These weekends have seen some excellent performances, including Albert Sidebottom conducting his own operetta, *The Parcel*, in 1981 and Malcolm Williamson's *The Happy Prince* the following year, and some fine solo performances from members of the First Orchestra. The 1980 performance of Benjamin Britten's *Noye's Fludde* in St Nicolas Church, Newbury, was a vast undertaking, with 160 pupils taking part as singers, instrumentalists, and dancers. Paul Risoe, who played Noah, may have

small but select group who walked proudly out of Chapel when it was time for choir practice. We had to do "housework" instead. I can't remember what this consisted of, but it was made rather unattractive so that one had to be a very keen non-singer to prefer it.'

Rosemary Kimmins joined the music staff of Downe House in 1978. 'At first I was a part-time piano teacher and then I became full-time. Class singing was an important part of the curriculum and to be a member of a choir was considered the ultimate musical achievement.

'In my first year I was asked to take over the Middle School Choir, an unenthusiastic group of girls, too young to audition for the exalted Choral and disdainful of the younger girls' choirs! I am not sure if it was my animated flailing of arms in an attempt to galvanise them into actually singing or Miss Lunn's eager support on the piano, but Thursday evenings soon became a time of enthusiastic music-making. This led to the choir's first triumph in the summer concert with a beautiful performance of Armstrong Gibbs' 'Silver'. From that moment a choir was born and for the next decade it continued to flourish and perform to the highest standard. Many of those choristers went on to become leading members of Choral where, under the expert guidance of Trevor Selby, Director of Choral Music, the singing was superb and the repertoire exciting and innovative.

Music in Jubilee Hall, above, and in the Cloisters, below

taught art, but he has a magnificent bass voice and took part in many productions.

'There have been many distinguished performers at concerts in Jubilee Hall, beginning with Myra Hess at the opening of the hall in 1958 and then Moura Lympany to inaugurate the new Steinway grand piano in 1988. Shortly afterwards John Lill came to give a recital on a grand piano that was delivered for him from Steinway's in

London. We were extremely pleased when he decided that he preferred our Steinway and gave a superb performance on it.

'As the number of pupils increased in the 1980s so did the number of music staff, and the number of pianos. We began a scheme to raise money to replace many of the old pianos and to fill empty cells and rooms, with brass plaques on the pianos recording the names of those who contributed. Over a few years we were able to buy twenty-five new pianos and several second-hand ones, much appreciated not just by the Downe House girls and staff but by the National Youth Orchestra who came to rehearse during the summer holidays for a few years.

'Many visiting music teachers – far too many to mention – have given long and loyal service to the important part that music has always played at Downe. Many full-time members of staff have been inspirational and long-serving. Albert Sidebottom in the 1970s and Trevor Selby in the 1980s and 1990s took Choral to tremendous heights with exciting and demanding repertoires which included all kinds of music from Purcell to the Beatles. Both men were composers in their own right, and also gifted arrangers of music –

Mr Sidebottom with the First Orchestra in Jubilee Hall, 1976

The Lower Fourth Choir at the finals of the National Choral Competition in 1989, conducted by Miss Byrom-Taylor with Miss Butcher as accompanist

often a difficult task when the only voices available are female. Cecilia Lunn joined for one day a week in 1964, but almost immediately became full-time and retired in 2001 after thirty-six years. She still does two and a half days at the school, giving individual lessons in piano and singing and working with the Remove Choir. Josephine Butcher spent twenty-five years at Downe House until her untimely death in 2002. She helped to guide numerous pupils through public examinations, conducted the First Orchestra, and organised hundreds of entries for the Associated Board examinations. She was a brilliant pianist and, fittingly, a new Bluthner piano given in her memory bears a small plaque recording her time at Downe House. Rosemary Evans was another accomplished organist, accompanist, and conductor, and taught many academic music classes.

'There are now teachers for all instruments and for solo singing, as well as six full-time music staff who share the class teaching, the orchestras, and the choirs, together with individual lessons. Most of the girls learn one or two instruments, which creates a huge timetabling challenge, for both lessons and practice!

'More pupils led to the formation of more choirs. The Remove Choir have been successful at many music festivals, particularly the Southampton Festival, and the Lower Fourth Choir also achieved spectacular success in 1989 when they reached the finals of the National Choral Competition and sang at the Royal Festival Hall.

'In 1982 a Choral Society of senior girls and some staff was formed, and 1984 saw our first collaboration with Radley College. Almost 300 singers and orchestral players took part, including in the chorus Downe's Headmistress, Suzanne Farr, and Radley's Warden, Denis Silk. Collaboration with other schools followed and of course the social aspect was very popular! We sang with Eton, Bradfield, Pangbourne, and Douai, and also did joint orchestral concerts and opera with Bradfield.

'The annual Music Competitions, including hotly contested House Competitions, have always been an important feature of Downe House musical life, and we have so many entries that preliminary rounds have to be held before a visiting adjudicator comes to judge the finals and award the trophies. Many ensembles also enter

national competition, with notable success.'

In the years since the arrival of Anthony Cain as Director of Music in 1992, the musical life of the school has broadened. While Choral and the orchestras have continued to excel, other groups of musicians have been established. A select Chamber Orchestra was formed and began the practice of touring annually in Scotland. The Wind Band, under the much-missed Jack Wilkinson, evolved via the Jazz Band into the Big Band. Middle School choir and the junior choirs were refigured into Repertory Choir for the Lower Fifth and a revived Junior Choral. The latter, resplendent in blue cassocks presented by the DHSA and directed by Stasio Sliwka, have followed the earlier practice of Choral tours with visits to Venice, while Choral itself has continued to tour: St Petersburg is the venue planned for centenary year.

Other innovations include the introduction by Stephanie Frankland of Piano Proms which, together with the Instrumental Proms begun later, have become a regular feature of Music Weekends. Lunchtime concerts by girls, staff, and visitors are very popular and the annual Prep School Orchestral Festival, hosted by Downe, is much enjoyed. The department has moved into the computer age, using software and keyboards, running composition workshops, and most recently introducing music technology as an A-level option. Yet the links with the past remain: each year the Hill Violin Bow, owned by Marjorie Gunn and presented to the school by her sister Sazzie after Miss Gunn's death, is presented to the most outstanding string player in the school. If she is a violinist, she may use the bow until it is handed over to her successor. It is named the Hill Bow in memory of Elizabeth Hill (Gardner), a talented pupil who became a professional violinist but died in an accident while still young.

As Miss Byrom-Taylor has written: 'People often say, "Downe House – that's a very musical school, isn't it?" Yes indeed!'

CHAPTER 4
A new beginning

Suzanne Farr

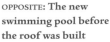
OPPOSITE: **The new swimming pool before the roof was built**

Miss Farr

The 1960s and 1970s was a time of accelerating change in the history of girls' education. The words 'equality of opportunity' were gaining urgency, and independent girls' schools began to take the lead in answering the call. Not only were curricula broadened to provide a greater range of subjects, but the raising of teacher and pupil expectations prompted many more girls, not only those rated clever, to stay on to take A-levels. At the same time, insistent demands from women themselves for well-paid careers, and the recognition that they offered valuable talents beyond those of child-rearing and domesticity, led to relentless and increasing pressure for places at university and for equal opportunities within employment. Girls and women were constantly challenged to prove their worth, and as they did so the walls of prejudice began to be broken down. The monstrous regiment was on the march!

This double decade was an exciting, heady time for anyone teaching in a girls' independent school worth its salt. The scope for widening the opportunities of the pupils was limited only by lack of the rich funds available to their boys' school counterparts from endowments and the much higher fees, which few fathers at that time would have paid for their daughters' education. The independent sector, in a strong position to recruit pupils because of the demise of most of the grammar schools, saw a division developing within girls' independent education itself. The great majority of schools, faced with the high cost of modernisation and the need to fund the new challenge to put girls on the map, chose to increase their numbers, particularly of those in the Sixth Form. A much greater choice of subjects for public examination necessitated taking on new staff, all earning recently increased teachers' salaries. Better science facilities needed to be built. In boarding schools dull weekends were being replaced by a myriad of clubs and activities, and the Physical Education programme had begun to encompass individual as well as team sports.

A staff/school lacrosse match captained by Miss Farr

96

It was clear that, by this time, the great majority of parents were beginning to realise that in choosing a good school for their daughters they were providing greatly enhanced opportunities for them. Rising numbers in the better Preparatory Schools soon began to reflect parents' determination to obtain a place for their daughters in the best school possible, which was not necessarily, as in the past, their mothers' *alma mater*. At the same time the knell was sounding for the few girls' schools unwilling or unable to respond to these changes – those which continued to give girls a genteel start in life, with a good background in the arts and few other advantages, except perhaps being surrounded by friends from a similar social stratum with some usefully eligible brothers.

During this time Downe House ceased to be one of the pioneers in the world of girls' education. Olive Willis had loathed the strictly regimented life of girls' boarding education of her time and had founded a school with a fine, independent spirit, which had moved ahead of those that were simply poor imitations of repressive boys' public schools. So strong was the loyal adherence to her principles

that over the years the school had become a time-warp, hardly aware of new and exciting advances being offered to girls elsewhere. Instead of maintaining its reputation as a leader in the field of girls' education, the school had begun to lag sadly behind. By 1978, with thirty empty beds and only fourteen names on the entry lists, closure was beginning to be a real possibility.

This was the nightmare I walked into after I had accepted the Governors' offer of the Headship. Only days later, I was phoned by Miss Mitchell, the Bursar, to be told the state of play. My tour of the school had taken me to the areas which could not fail to impress: the Chapel, Jubilee Hall, the impeccably run Sanatorium, the Library with its portrait of Olive Willis. I hardly saw a pupil, but I did see a very attractive campus in a wonderfully accessible location. I was assured that the school, although needing some changes, was in a strong position financially. In reality it appeared that only a miracle could save it.

I shall never forget my first meeting with the whole school. I was told by my kind and efficient secretary, Susi Maxwell Knight, that it was customary for the Head to have supper with the girls on the first evening. I made my way to the Dining Room to find that I had been placed on the High, completely alone. The meal was conducted in chaos: screaming girls, food flying about the room, and a rapid realisation of what I was up against. There were no teaching Housemistresses there to give me support, to show an interest in the girls, or to see that new girls were being properly looked after. This superb race of people who work long hours every day to see that boarding schools are happy, caring places for their charges, as well as engineering opportunities for enormously useful social development, had remained, by tradition, excluded from Downe House. An increasingly desperate need for them had always been ignored.

What did I do about the bedlam? Sheer fury took over and, with a voice well-developed on lacrosse pitches to rise above noise, I obtained a surprised silence. I quite simply told the girls that I had never dined with people like them in my life and didn't intend to start now. Suddenly they became perfectly pleasant, likeable schoolgirls and we all continued with the meal, though I think we were all more than a little shell-shocked.

I went back to Hill House that night realising in alarm that I had left most of the girls in the school in the main building, with no professional staff to supervise them other than matrons with very little status and therefore no power, and no established House hierarchy of older girls as back-up. I suspected, and was proved right when a fire-practice was held, that there was no workable system for evacuating the buildings in case of fire. I paced through the almost empty, bleak Hill House (furniture had not been provided and the new carpets and curtains in three of the twelve rooms I was inhabiting were all a depressing brown) wondering how soon a House system could be introduced. The school had to increase in size, but only if Houses could be introduced. I could sense the wrath of Olive Willis and genera-tions of Old Seniors swirling round me as I con-templated such treachery.

Consolation came quickly the next day when, to my great joy, I discovered that I had the support of a most remarkable collection of Seniors from a small Upper Sixth Form. These wise, mature girls were respected by most of the other girls and had been virtually holding the school together for the last couple of terms in the face of some particu-larly unpleasant thuggery from a few unhappy and manipulative pupils. I also discovered, from the moment that the staff came in to school the next morning, that there were enclaves of excellent teaching in some subjects, and that many of the staff were keen to get things right quickly, though few were aware of the desperately pressing need for new pupils. Elizabeth Doherty, who was then Deputy Head, was a first-rate support, full of good sense and with a wonderful sense of humour. While we could still laugh it was all bearable!

Ballroom dancing with Bradfield was the highlight of the week. On a Monday evening we would all pile into the coach, donning eye liner and lip gloss *en route*, and be taken the nine miles to Bradfield where we were shown how to waltz gracefully around the room, accompanied by much hysterical giggling. Many a relationship was formed in that gym in Bradfield, and many a heart broken. Later, my boyfriend and another chap cycled over from Bradfield to see me one Saturday afternoon, and I had to hide them from Mrs Doherty. She knew that there were some 'Braddy laddies' there but couldn't find them. Many a time we had close shaves, with boys hiding in cupboards – it was all terribly innocent, but quite thrilling at the time!

Anna Markwell (1980)

We arrived as Removes in our green djibbahs and desert boots. There was a steep learning curve: 'running' – a ghastly task as your table of terrifying older girls relied on you to dash to the kitchen hatch as soon as Grace had finished to bring back food as quickly as possible; 'wandering' when your table was full and you had to beg a seat somewhere else. Then we had to negotiate the embarrassment of choosing a 'pash', an older girl to have a crush on. As a 'satellite', our duties included running the odd errand and making her bed, and in return we occasionally got given Mars bars.

Later in the Middle Fourths work became more serious and there was the horror of 'mark reading' when your weekly mark and position were read out in class. However, there was always comfort in food such as 'sticky willies' (iced buns). Lower Sixth year brought ballroom dancing lessons at Bradfield with the 'laddies', with the possibility of meeting the 'Braddy laddies' the following Sunday at Bucklebury Ford which was firmly out of bounds.

Alex Birnie, Bridget Campbell, Melanie Denham-Davies, Nicky Fazakerley, Diana Ffennell (1980)

The Governors, with Baroness Warnock as Chairman, conceded that more care was needed for the girls, and at the end of the first term the introduction of the House system was announced. Frank Shaw, the former Headmaster of King's College School, Wimbledon, gave me generous support from the outset, and Pamela Barnett gave even braver encouragement, since she and her two

97

A new girl's initiation into Downe House life in the Michaelmas term was via the 'Bumps'. Girls would cycle off out of the school gates in sensible groups of three. Slipping off the road onto a track strewn thick with copper leaves, the new girl soon found herself deep in the woods, chasing over and under high banks and dips. Pedalling hard to keep up with this exhilarating and newfound freedom, and just when she might panic with the thought that the others had abandoned her, she reached the final summit – and new friends leapt from the trees and christened the new girl in leaves. Beautiful – and tame and innocent! The Bumps were just one of many carefree adventurous places to explore.

Annabel Gray (Ludovici, 1983)

I have memories of bicycling for miles at weekends through the woods around Cold Ash, following the paths through the woods amidst the glorious autumn colours. The freedom was wonderful after being at school all week. We would also go miles to a field where corn cobs were grown for cattle feed, from where we would bring cobs back to school and cook them using boilettes in the piano practice cells.

Camilla Rigall (Belloc-Lowndes, 1983)

sisters had both experienced the delights of Downe without Houses. Jacqueline Bartrum's and Kit Russell's enthusiasm for the new plans was worth more than gold, for as Secretary and Chairman of the Seniors' Association their influence was far-reaching. Such trust in a new and inexperienced Head meant a great deal.

My plan for chopping the school up into five discrete House areas, the making of flats for House staff and their families from dormitory space, the naming of the Houses after Miss Willis's own homes, streets, or villages, and the employment of suitable House staff all went through on the nod and we had an embryonic House system by the next term. Some brave staff, notably Barbara Sidebottom, offered to become the first pioneering, resident House staff, bringing husbands and in some cases family with them. In the care of Barbara Sidebottom, supported by her husband Albert, then Director of Music, Tedworth was very much a trail-blazing House. We had employed two intrepid builders, who worked throughout the Christmas holidays breaking down walls in the South Rooms to create the necessary living space and a flat for the House staff. They came back twice with revised estimates because they had found it almost impossible to break through walls constructed from Miss Nickel's own precursor of the breeze block.

Juliet Austin also volunteered to come in to take charge of Ancren Gate, bringing her husband Anthony and daughter Elizabeth with her. As Miss Willis's great-niece she was a link between old and new Downe. These hugely supportive husbands were quite a feature of my time at Downe. They were friendly and fun, brisk in their approach to any girlish stupidity, and often very ready to run a hobby group; Anthony Austin was in charge of Beekeeping. They were especially good at putting bumptious or impertinent youngsters smartly on the right tracks. Some girls were rather surprised that there seemed to be an adult consensus about what was regarded as acceptable behaviour.

The girls were in the main intrigued and excited by the changes in the school. House loyalty began to grow from the first, but establishing the idea in their minds that there were two members of staff living with them who were there as supports, consultants, advocates, and on occasion defenders seemed a wholly foreign idea. Only gradually was the trust necessary for such a normal relationship established. The first House lacrosse matches were played soon after, and Cold Ash village residents were astounded at the volume and urgency of the cheering. I couldn't resist a smile when I heard it from the Drawing Room for the first time. It was an enthusiastic sound from a school that had previously abhorred House competition.

The House staff and I met constantly to hammer out everything from a workable laundry system to agreed bedtimes and the finer points of exeats. Above all, we had to be sure that the Houses were administered fairly. Planning and

Finding things to keep us occupied at the weekends was sometimes quite a challenge. Like all teenage girls, we spent a lot of time preening ourselves and experimenting with make-up, outfits, and weird hairstyles, plus the odd ear piercing that usually went septic. For what? We had nowhere to go and no boys to impress. One weekend about five or six of us set off for a bike ride, all dressed up to the nines. A few miles from the school we found a field with a huge mound of silage covered in black industrial polythene held down with old tyres. This seemed a perfect place to play, so we set about chasing each other and tottering all over it in our stilettos, oblivious to the damage our shoes were doing to the silage under the airtight plastic. The next thing was a furious farmer running towards us cursing and shouting. We tore off on our bikes in what we thought was a successful getaway, until to our horror that evening Mrs Doherty announced that she'd been contacted by a local farmer about serious damage to his property and that the girls responsible should own up. The farmer had clearly had no difficulty in recognising where the curiously dressed girls had come from! We had no choice but to admit to our childish crime and face Miss Farr, our parents, and a large bill from the farmer, for several hundred pounds. For me the consequence was the whole Christmas holidays without any parties. For Annabel Gray (Ludovici, 1983), the result was the sale of her little grey pony.

Jane Tahourdin (Haughton, 1983)

100

We were the 'girls on the hill' – and people still say that rather dreamily when you mention where you went to school. We were the last to wear djibbahs, a fantastic warm creation with desert boots, and cloaks with so many rotten name tapes in them that you never really worked out who owned them. They came from the second-hand box in the gallery above the Dining Room. We were also allowed to make our own summer djibbahs, so my mother made yellow and purple ones, which infuriated Miss Farr as generally of course they were pink and green. Changing to summer djibbahs coincided with the announcement at lunch that we would be able to walk on the grass as well until further notice. Why was that so exciting? But it was!

Emma McGrigor (Fellowes, 1983)

implementing it all was demanding, but we had the huge advantage of having seen many other boarding-school House systems in operation, and we knew which good ideas to glean or remodel. By far our greatest advantage was being able to offer flats of reasonable size to married House staff and their children. Many other girls' boarding schools had been purpose-built to allow a Housemistress only a sitting room with an adjacent bedroom. Amazingly, this system had persisted until the 1980s when House staff without family attached became impossible to find. We experienced no such difficulty.

Antipathy towards the House system from some Old Seniors, as a betrayal of the founding principles, was often vehemently expressed, especially, and understandably, from those who had daughters in the school and had looked for an educational philosophy similar to that which they themselves had experienced. Never, however, was a pudding more effectively proved in the eating, for as the House system gradually began to flourish they found that, with two welcoming and kindly teaching Housemistresses in every House, there was always someone who knew their daughters well with whom to discuss all kinds of problems. One mother even poured out her distress at her impending divorce to a slightly surprised House-

OPPOSITE: **Hill House**

mistress, but nonetheless received just as much tea and sympathy as her daughter would have done. The teaching staff, who in the past had individually stepped into the breach when a child was distressed, were perhaps a little sad that these troubles were now most often being recognised and looked after in-House; but they were encouraged to join in the pastoral care by being attached to Houses themselves and by passing on any concerns about girls they taught to House staff, always ready to listen.

The dissenters among the girls were soon eased out of their opposition as the mixed-age groups began to work together on all kinds of activities. Fortunately Downe House had always had a tradition of mixed-age bedrooms and had no rigid age-based Houses to replace. This easy ability to mix with all ages was a considerable advantage to us. A few diehards, desperately clutching at tradition, also objected when we decided to brighten up the drab green uniform by introducing, in 1979, a choice of red or green pullovers, striped blazers, and a longer, warmer cloak. They were all for a return to the djibbah (a few had survived among those about to leave), but when I pointed out that they were not a Downe invention at all, but had been imported from Roedean, their objections ceased.

Some unusual benefits accrued from the changes. A huge number of girls were learning flute when I arrived because, as well as being a gifted teacher, Hilary Finzi was also a sympathetic listener. Once she was less in demand for consolation and advice, the range of instruments available for the orchestra grew and our already well-founded music reputation flourished so well that eventually a second orchestra was needed. So many girls were eventually learning two instruments, and so determined was I that girls should no longer leave academic lessons for their music teaching, that only the combined administrative wizardry of Valerie Byrom Taylor and Josephine Butcher could have devised a workable music timetable for the whole school at the start of the school year, and have continued to make on-the-spot revisions. It was a magnificent annual accomplishment, enabling many girls to enjoy their music to a high standard while carrying a busy academic programme.

From the first my life in school seemed to lurch between triumph and disaster. A young pupil died from pneumonia in my first Christmas holidays, and I can still recall the feeling of utter desolation at the funeral service at Stoke Poges. This was my first experience of the death of a pupil in all my time in boarding schools. Also in the first term, girls were found missing from their beds by the Seniors, who with considerable wisdom and maturity came over to Hill House to alert me: not at all an easy thing to do. These kind girls stayed with me until the miscreants returned in the early hours. The Governors and I knew that we had to empty even more beds in order to take a stand against such foolishness.

Birthdays

As described by Annabel Gray (Ludovici, 1983), 'Having a birthday at Downe was really not such a rough ordeal. The night before your day, your 'room' would take round a 'Wacky-B' to all the rooms in every house. This was a wastepaper basket filled to the brim with everything a girl could possible need, mostly writing paper, envelopes, and stamps, the most prized paper being Hunky Dory. Perhaps four Wacky-Bs would arrive on your bed early in the morning and a group would crowd round eagerly watching every donation being unpacked and sorted. Down to breakfast and more to follow: hundreds of girls singing 'Happy Birthday'. The table at which the birthday girl was seated would sing the first line, then the neighbouring table would sing the line, and so it went clockwise round the Dining Room until each table had sung the complete song. The overall effect was something like a football stadium, and no amount of hushing from house matrons could keep the roof on. The finale was even more deafening as every girl banged her olive green plastic cup and saucer on the table to a primeval rhythm (no rhythm at all!) and in one final gesture flung saucers high up into the open gallery above, to more cheering and continued delight. Everyone joined in, even the most subdued and studious girls. Marvellous!'

Fifth Form leaving dares

One of the most spectacular of these is remembered by all those who were at the school at the time (1978). Anna Markwell (1980) was involved: 'At five o'clock one summer's morning in 1978, we physically lifted a Mini belonging to Miss Horsburgh (history teacher, who can't have been much older than us) from the front of the main entrance, up the steps and through the arch to Chapel, then down the steps on the other side to the terrace in front of the Staff Common Room. On top of the car we placed a papier maché peanut (her nickname), with a sign saying "Go to work on a peanut". All this was done with tremendous care and control – the car was covered in blankets and lifted (goodness knows how!) by our year. Not a scratch or a speck of dirt was to be seen!'

Alexandra Griffiths (Squires, 1977) remembers her year's leaving joke, which was 'to empty the Dining Room completely in the early hours of the morning and to lay it out, with all the tables in exactly the same position, on the grass just outside so that everyone knew where their tables were when they came down for breakfast.'

Then came a wonderful helping hand from Wycombe Abbey, where the lists were greatly over-subscribed. Hearing of emerging changes, Patricia Lancaster, the Head, agreed to divert parents towards Downe to look at what we were doing. Most of those who came had enough faith in us to send their daughters and they, with other talented children, formed the nucleus of the first larger intake of girls at eleven, all of whom would be able to stay on for A-levels. God was most certainly on our side, for they were the most multi-talented group I have ever seen within one year. They formed our first separate Junior School. Pat

Lancaster and I became good friends, but there were times when I couldn't resist teasing her about the rich abundance of talent she had diverted in our direction.

As the tempo of school life increased, we found two new homes for the Junior School eleven-year-olds by creating a smaller Sanatorium and a much smaller house for me down at St Peter's, releasing what became Darwin and Hill House for the youngsters. It was a great joy to see them playing in the woods around their Houses instead of being trapped up on the top floor in the main building. A rather ungrateful move was to pinch one of Wycombe

Abbey's most successful Housemistresses, Lynne Berwick, to head the Junior School, but we didn't feel too badly about it! St Peter's became more like home for me, even though it took a little time for it to be redecorated. My lovely daily help, Maud Pocock, already in her eighties and a former maid to Miss Willis, did her best to make me comfortable and to console my Cocker Spaniel and three Irish Setters for my long absences. A devoted dog lover, Maud was in her element and the housework came a long way second. Once when I was preparing to fly up to school, leaving her with apologies for the chaos, she said in her utterly forthright way, 'You are just like Miss Willis, she was untidy too!' I didn't know if this was meant to be a compliment or an admonishment.

Physical Education on the wastes of the games fields was not popular, the gym was far too small for strenuous activity, and the swimming pool, attractively set amongst the pine trees, delivered a dose of pine needles laced with weed to any swimmer silly enough to breathe with accepted racing technique. Something had to be done about the general fitness of the school. The Governors were far-sighted and trusting in allowing steadily-filling coffers to fund an indoor swimming pool and three glass-walled squash courts. A beautiful design by the Winchester College architect, who to my delight and relief wanted to echo the Downe House round arch theme, gave us a beautiful building which not only blended into our attractive campus but was reminiscent of Miss Nickel's elegant galleried Dining Room. Although my primary aim was to raise academic standards and motivation generally, so that a university or specialist education became a realistic choice for all our pupils, it was the swimming pool which proved to be an important milestone along the way. Not only did it give us a healthier, more vigorous school, but a more confident one. The girls were proud of owning a facility better than any other girls' school and I think they realised at that point that the many promises were actually going to come true.

I remember – rather too vividly – streaking in my first summer term. I can't think why we decided to do it and who the other girls were, but each of us entered one of the cells fully clothed, waited for the signal, and emerged naked to race across the Cloisters and back. We were caught committing this fearful transgression by a Senior and reported – wretched girl, where was her sense of fun? All my other memories involve activities which are, frankly, not fit for general consumption. But my best friends are old Downe House girls, which pretty much says it all.

Rachel Willis Fleming (Hollins, 1983)

I remember the Interflora van arriving for me on my birthday. And playing the 'Last Post' on Remembrance Sunday in Chapel in my last year. Before that it was always Nico Finzi, who was a genius trumpeter, but she had left so Mr Kellow (brilliant teacher) let me do it. Not being quite up to Nico's standard I fluffed the top G which was a shame, but I really enjoyed the experience.

Rebecca Stevenson (1986)

Miss Wheaton in action

Outdoor gym, 1981

Judith Wheaton very quickly restored order and a more self-critical attitude to performance in Physical Education, and in her care the teams were always immaculately turned out. After she was joined in the department by two young England squad players the standard of lacrosse soared, while the Houses achieved an amazingly high standard in the annual House gymnastic competition, despite the severe restrictions of such a small and oddly-shaped gymnasium. The success achieved on the lacrosse field was of particular importance to me because my own college lacrosse coach had been a Downe House Senior, Isabel Nowell-Smith. I was out to prove that Downe was a top lacrosse school.

As confidence within and outside the school grew, we began to attract girls into the Sixth Form and more of our own stayed on. This created a need for a boarding house where our Upper Sixth could begin adapting to a life more akin to that of a student. Now that a steadily increasing intake was bringing in a reassuring fees surplus, we felt confident enough in ourselves to launch an appeal for additional funds for building the new house. By then we were wisely guided on the Finance Committee by Peter Grant and James Tyrrell, Deputy Director of Lazards and Finance Director of Abbey National respectively, and Jeremy Francis, then Financial Director of a large supermarket chain. It would have been easy to squander in a random fashion our new influx of funds and these three kept my feet on *terra firma*, my ideas securely harnessed to the master plan, and the school on an excellent financial footing.

They were aided by Patrick Maclure who, as an absolutely indefatigable Bursar, was the improvising wizard behind nearly all the adaptations to the buildings. The more outlandish the task I set him, the more stalwart was his response; but he must truly have dreaded our weekly meetings, wondering what on earth was coming next. On one occasion an extreme need for more sitting-room space in Tedworth caused me to suggest that an adjacent bicycle shed might be appropriated. After only one short school holiday Tedworth found itself with a warm, attractively appointed common room with not a bicycle in sight. Patrick's marvellous sense of humour certainly put oil on the cog wheels. He had a habit of ringing across from the Bursary with the best of the after-dinner jokes from his MCC dinners, and on one occasion his telephone call coincided with an afternoon interview with prospective parents. I had to receive an urgent message from the Bursar with an absolutely straight face – all the more difficult because the joke was outrageously funny.

Whatever their misgivings about the House system, the members of the Seniors' Association responded magnificently to the appeal for an Upper Sixth Form House, making it possible to go ahead with little delay. I remember jubilantly taking a letter from Laura Aitken, a past Head Senior, down to the Staff Room with its enclosure of a £10,000 cheque from the Beaverbrook Trust.

**The bursar,
Patrick Maclure**

It was a lot of money in those days and certainly prompted others to give generously. We were also hugely grateful to Evelyn Barbirolli, who as Evelyn Rothwell had begun her musical life as a small girl at Downe and was later to win international acclaim as an oboist, for the concert she gave to raise funds for the appeal. I hope some of her reward came when our talented Under Sixteen

The best thing about doing French A-level was that we were all allowed to subscribe to *Paris Match*. The intention, of course, was to improve our French vocabulary relating to the important current events of the day; the reality was hours spent in the library poring over the love lives of Princesses Caroline and Stephanie, Alain Delon, and the like, and learning about French fashion and cinema. Far more useful, of course!

I have strong memories of the complicated pecking order for seating in the very small TV area in the attic in Aisholt. Television was a fairly restricted activity, and was always interrupted by more senior girls turning up and the whole room having to reseat itself in accordance with the unwritten code that meant that the more senior sat on the sofa in the middle, with the rest spread around accordingly. Woe betide you if you didn't offer up your seat and move when someone older appeared in the room.

Phyllida Middlemiss (Cheyne, 1986)

There's a man in the House

Barbara Sidebottom was the first Housemistress of Tedworth; her husband, Albert, was Director of Music. The following is taken from Tedworth House *Magazine*:

When the history of Downe House is written, the date January 14th 1979 will appear in very large letters. On this day a man took up residence within that bastion of female exclusivity. Middle and Bottom South became Tedworth and a special corner of it was converted into quarters suitably superior and luxurious. This is how it was!

The first few days are critical. How is it going to work out? What will happen if I meet HIM in the corridor on the way back from the bathroom when I am clad only in a towel?

For a time he is conspicuous by his absence. Perhaps he will never appear in the house? Is he too shy, do you think? But gradually, little by little, there are signs of a more enlightened attitude. Occasionally he strides down the corridor, looking neither to left nor to right. Then comes the breakthrough! He is invited (yes, invited) into a Sixth Form bedroom in order to fit a draught excluder to the window. What a feeble excuse. Coffee is prepared in one of the (now banned) boilettes and there he is, as large as life, sitting on a bed at 9.30pm, drinking coffee.

History is made and the flag is run up the flagpole.

Now, of course, the novelty has worn off. If we meet him on the way to the bathroom we hitch up our towels and give him a bright smile. Not so, however, in the other houses! We hear that one evening he had to venture into foreign territory on a matter of some urgency (actually a false fire alarm), to be greeted by a wave of mild hysteria. Rumour has it that other men are to become resident in the houses, with their wives, of course! We wonder whether any of them will have interesting sons.

Mr Sidebottom conducting *Noye's Fludde*

Group won the National Schools Chamber Music competition. Incognito in their own clothes, they collected their prizes from an unsuspecting Chairman of the Judges, Lady Barbirolli. Her delight was plain to see when she discovered where they came from.

With funds assured, we found a firm in Surrey who had developed a method of constructing timber-framed buildings, whereby the frame arrived already assembled with the brickwork and

roof to be added later. I stood in the window of the School Secretary's Office above the front door to watch so-called New House, a jerry-built house next to the Laundry, being pushed over with little effort by bulldozers to make room for the first York House. The demise of New House erased some unhappy memories of when I had been summoned to the school soon after my appointment to try to persuade the Upper Fifth to stay on. Intent on staging a mass exodus, the girls met me in New

when the Upper Sixth would take up residence. We sat around York on the grass, in bright sunshine, happily putting together desks, tables, chests, and bookcases from the cardboard boxes strewn around us. A flat-pack plan is a great leveller amongst the intelligentsia, and it caused much hilarity when two much-respected members of the English department solemnly constructed a large bookcase, which was then found to be far too large to go through any of the doors. The bedrooms were papered by end-of-line rolls from the Laura Ashley factory's winter sale in mid-Wales; a great day out for me. I was determined that the house should be pretty, feminine, and most of all unschooly, and with Laura Ashley in vogue this wasn't difficult to achieve. There were no graffiti in this house nor, as we began to redecorate all the Houses, did they reappear: another battle won.

The formal opening of York House provided a precious memory to salt away. Dame Rosemary Murray, an Old Senior, Principal of New Hall, and the first woman Vice-Chancellor of Cambridge University, was invited to open the House.

York House, right, opened in 1981 by Dame Rosemary Murray, above

House with some resentful faces, in a room full of battered armchairs and a strong smell of cats.

I stood at that same window, not long after, to see the skeleton of York House, complete with insulated infill panels, rise from the base in a single day like a giant doll's house. We suddenly had a Sixth Form House, and we were very much in business. A kind offer from Sir Terence Conran, whose daughter was at the school, to supply furniture for York House at a very much reduced price allowed us to go on a heady spending spree to Habitat's Wallingford headquarters. The staff were invited to come to a picnic-cum-furniture-assembly party before the start of the Michaelmas term

Sport

Alice Carver, Olive Willis's first partner, was a member and later captain of the England women's hockey team, so sport had its place at Downe House from the very beginning. Hockey and cricket teams were soon established, to be followed by lacrosse (always in the early days known as 'crosse'). One of the pupils at Downe during the early years was Audrey Lucas, daughter of E V Lucas, and so in 1913 the annual *Punch* cricket match was played at the school between E V Lucas's eleven and Sir James Barrie's eleven. The result is not recorded, but one of the players, A A Milne, was remembered as twisting his ankle in trying to leap nonchalantly over a fence.

An inspection in the 1930s records four periods of gym and one of dancing a week, together with games played every day except Sunday. The girls did all this in their djibbahs in the early decades. Dance – known as 'floppy dancing' – came into the curriculum in the late 1930s and remained part of the school's activities until the 1960s. Nicola FitzGerald (Norman-Butler, 1957) remembers 'floppy dancing – a type of Isadora Duncan free movement, not conducive

The gym in the 1920s, left; the Gym VI in 1930, top; massed outdoor gym rehearsal in 1942, above

Floppy dancing

to fat teenagers, wearing our coloured summer tunics.' Its beginnings at the school are remembered by Valerie Preston Dunlop (Preston, 1946): 'Not only was 'floppy dancing' taught throughout the school, including the Sixth Form and Seniors, but it was immensely popular and a regular part of the summer demonstrations in the Cloisters. It was European Modern Dance, which was not about pointing your toes, but creative, and led us into intense expression of serious themes.'

Brenda Artus (Touche, 1950) was captain of the Downe House cricket team in 1950, when a home match was arranged against Marlborough boys. 'When they came, I was shocked to find that five of my eleven were expected to play on the boys' side and I was expected to have five of them. Fortunately I had two excellent cricketers, Sally Haggard and Elizabeth Jukes, both of whom had learned to play cricket from

The new swimming pool with its roof in place

the age of seven at the boys' prep schools where their fathers had taught. Elizabeth was a fearsome left-arm bowler, and of course I kept them both in my side along with the best of the rest. When it came near the end, our teacher suggested that I put myself on to bowl, although my bowling was rather pathetic – and by some fluke my second ball hit the stumps . . . and we had won! I don't think they stayed for tea!'

The unheated outdoor swimming pool, set among the pines, was not always an attractive prospect, as it was usually covered with slime and pine needles and was the haunt of frogs. Pearl Brewis (Beaumont-Thomas, 1938) recalls 'the swimming pool covered with thick green slime which I refused to dive through, but was made to once when it was threatened that my whole class would be taken off swimming if I didn't.' Gillian Richards (Taylor, 1967), along with several others

of her era, remembers 'Miss Maclean (Mamie), who taught piano and who, we were led to believe, was in her seventies and had been an Olympic swimmer. At the end of the swimming sports we were treated to a diving exhibition, and she fascinated us because she kept her make-up on and had to dab it dry every time she came out of the water, so I'm afraid to say we noticed more about that than her very neat dives.' Those willing to brave the danger, and the pool itself, went for illicit midnight swims. On one such occasion Geraldine James (Thomas, 1968) recalls 'suddenly seeing the glow of a cigarette through the trees and knowing it was Nancy Medley watching us. She didn't need to say anything – we just fled!'

A new indoor swimming pool was built soon after Miss Farr's arrival, together with squash courts and a new gym. Individual sports, as well

as the traditional team games, began to become available. Miss Farr, herself a former member of the England lacrosse team, was determined to make Downe a top lacrosse school, and some of the pupils who joined the school during and after her time have helped to build and sustain that vision. Judith Wheaton was a charismatic Head of the sports department at this time. Few who were there then will forget her masterly organisation of the annual school photo, as well as her insistence on immaculate turn-out, both on and off the sports arenas. She organised successive teams of enthusiastic, talented games staff who encouraged the girls to do their best and to take pride in their skills and achievements. Lacrosse, tennis, swimming, squash, athletics, and gymnastics predominated, but aerobics, golf, cross-country running, and dance also had their enthusiasts. Paula Machin (Pritchard) trained the girls for sub-aqua and lifesaving qualifications as well as helping them to attain greater heights in swimming and diving, and at the same time John Payne produced keen squash players who soon reached the standards required for competing in national championships. The less athletic were encouraged to train and excel in other areas; one such was delighted (and amazed) to win her first ever sports trophy – for tennis umpiring.

Miss Wheaton's successors, Sarah Butt

(Richardson) and Lydia Rayne, respectively former England and Scotland lacrosse players, have broadened the possibilities available while still maintaining the high standards reached in the main sports. At the time of writing, the school holds the National Championship at both first team and under-fifteen level (shared with Guildford High School), the first time a school has ever held the double. Netball and hockey have become popular and successful too, and the

The McCosh girls: a major lacrosse family both at Downe and at international level; Pippa and Lizzy, top, represented England, while Diane and Caroline, above, played for Scotland

hockey teams in particular, composed of girls coming into the Upper Fourth from hockey-playing prep schools, are rapidly making their mark in national competitions.

Gymnastics and dance have moved with the times. Massed outdoor displays of gym and floppy dancing may have gone, but the annual gym competition, now in the new Sports Hall, is keenly fought over by the Houses while modern dance enthusiasts rejoice in their new studio. The annual Athletics Sports Day has become an important fixture in the school calendar, and many girls still follow their own interests and continue to row, sail, ride, and fence.

Clare Balding opening the Farr Centre in 2004

Afterwards she related a marvellous story of the school in her time: being of a practical turn of mind, she was often invited to accompany Miss Nickel on maintenance missions at the new school at Cold Ash, and once found herself being led up to the roof behind some chimney pots to hand Miss Nickel tools to effect roof repairs. She was amused to hear that the first York House would soon need to acquire a mirror image, such was the pressure for places, but was doubtful about the urgency of a new Science School, a project especially close to my heart. In her opinion, the quality of the teaching was paramount and learning chemistry in a shed at the early Downe House in Kent hadn't stood in her way. It certainly didn't seem so.

There are so many memorable milestones, and comic as well as serious reminders of the infinite variety of school life, that I can recount only a selection. I remember a group of Middle School musicians winning a Department of Trade and Industry competition for the most original use for a computer. They designed a database of sheet music, which could be sorted in a number of ways to allow musicians to find music appropriate to their needs. The prize was a BBC Acorn Computer, the first of many at Downe House. Increasing numbers of girls wishing to learn two instruments alongside a demanding academic schedule gave me particular pleasure. As a Housemistress in another life, I had spent many long hours trying to persuade clever girls that the dual advantage of their own intellectual strengths and the extra time afforded by boarding school should allow them to maintain interests beyond their A-level programmes. I know that in the main this advice fell on deaf ears and I vowed then that, if ever I became a Head, I would endeavour to create a more balanced attitude to learning, with achievement in several areas complementing and enhancing each other. Recent developments in education where league tables have been allowed to dominate the Sixth Form, narrowing and limiting the range of knowledge and experience and completely failing to prepare girls

Mrs Morgan was our maths teacher – a formidable lady with grey hair in a bun and a stern manner. She wore a huge anorak permanently, even in the hottest weather, and none of us had ever seen her without it. Underneath the anorak and stern face, however, was a soft heart of gold and this broke through with a long smile one warm summer's day. One of the class had, rather daringly, asked Mrs Morgan why she never took her anorak off. 'It's because it's got lots of useful pockets where I can hide pens, chalk, and board rubbers,' was the answer. We couldn't argue with that and the lesson continued as normal. A week later, double maths and the girl who had asked about the anorak stood up and announced that she had a present for the teacher. She had sewn a long piece of material with large pouches at each end and she walked up to the front of the class and presented Mrs Morgan with her new pockets, so that she wouldn't now have to keep her anorak on in hot weather. Mrs Morgan, momentarily speechless, slowly removed her anorak and spent the rest of the lesson with the new pockets hung around her neck.

I was Head of Choral in my final year, and it was the pinnacle of my ambitions at Downe. I took the role very seriously and was determined to make this Choral one of the best ever. One Sunday morning it was very hot. Choral all met in the narrow passage behind Chapel to don our cassocks, and as it was so hot we all stripped down to our underwear and put the cassocks on over the top. During the service we undid a few top buttons and slipped off our shoes to get some cooler air, but we remained demure choir-girls. Then when Miss Farr got to the lectern for the sermon, she announced that as it was so hot, for that occasion only, she would let Choral take their cassocks off for the rest of the service. We all looked at each other in horror, and I shifted around nervously and mumbled that we were all absolutely fine, really! Miss Farr looked completely mystified as she looked at her bunch of clearly very hot, sweaty singers, but went on to the rest of the service. Luckily she saw the funny side when we explained afterwards.

Elizabeth Gray (1987)

113

for the way they will have to juggle successfully several facets of their lives in adulthood, have been in my view a severely retrogressive step.

One of our early and rather adventurous innovations was to allow able girls to take some GCE (later GCSE) subjects a year early, allowing them more time for a wider programme. Results were good and A grades plentiful. Barbara Castellini produced the final vindication for the decision when her First Division French candidates all achieved A grades. From this strong Modern Languages department, headed so successfully by Elizabeth Owen, I had quietly and confidently waited for just such a result, but nevertheless it was a sturdy cornerstone in the building of academic confidence (A* grades had, of course, not been introduced at that stage, and A grades were highly prized).

Early in its life Holcombe House found themselves with a Housemaster and his wife, Jack and Angela Bayliss, in charge. Jack Bayliss was not only influential in the House scene but a revered and successful Head of History. They later moved to York House, where girls in their A-level year found that his interest and encouragement proved the mainspring of the stability and good sense they needed at a testing time. Angela also became a School Secretary of long-standing and immense value. Completely unflappable and a superb organiser, she bestowed quiet, calm deliberation on many a series of mini-crises, mostly caused in my time by a Head with fingers in too many pies. Soon after, Aisholt was to benefit from Eileen Houghton's wise guidance and unshakable standards. The Drawing Room, in daily use as my study, was in the middle of her House (not every Housemistress's idea of heaven!) and I knew at first hand that things were going well. The girls rose to her demands for the very best, and Aisholt became well known for the calibre of its Lower Sixth Form girls. Lynne Berwick's successor, Mary Moore, coming to us after a time at Westonbirt, carried on the lively educational tradition which had been established, with her own brand of wisdom laced with a great sense of fun. In her care the Junior School flourished as a happy but stimulating first step into boarding school life. The long and highly skilled service which these members of staff gave to Downe House ensures that their names will go down in history as the founders of the House system.

To my mind, a good general education has to accompany increasing specialisation. I introduced a lecture programme for Tuesday evenings after supper – which came to be known rather wryly as 'Compulsory Culture'! We managed to attract a good variety of speakers, and some riveting evenings resulted. I remember Sir Ranulf Fiennes, still with his greatest adventures and conquests ahead of him, prefacing his lecture with tales of his night-time visits to Downe House as a schoolboy, which apparently provided some of his early climbing experience too! Virginia Bottomley gave us a lively description of the difficulties facing women MPs in a male-oriented House of Commons, but to my regret it did not inspire any of the audience to seek out a career in politics. A high-flying woman barrister successfully scuppered my intention to project some girls towards the upper echelons of the law by telling the Sixth Form that, with hindsight, she would have stayed at home to look after her daughter herself, leaving career aspirations to one side and probably forsaking her place on the career ladder.

Not all lecturers held our attention. Two hours on the finer technicalities of 'Raising the Mary Rose' brought us at length to 'time for questions'. Not a hand went up, save for one in the front row containing a very drowsy Junior School. 'Do you feel,' asked the brave questioner, 'that it was ALL worth it?' Out of the mouths . . .

I have always believed that the friendship of animals can give a good deal of happiness to human beings. Their proper care can prevent self-absorbed youngsters from becoming too self-centred, and there was some danger that our girls could suffer from this when so much was being given to them. I therefore brought with me dual-purpose Ryeland sheep from my flock in Herefordshire, to provide the nucleus of our Young Farmers Club and to become grass mowers for the untidy land around St Peter's. Most of the Club members came from London homes, for whom getting up early on a frosty morning to replenish the hay racks was a novel experience. Archie the ram was brought up to the Hobbies Fair in Jubilee Hall at the start of the Michaelmas term as a visual aid to advertise the Club, and fortunately behaved impeccably. He also allowed himself to be shampooed by his young caretakers preparing him in St Peter's garden for the Newbury Show. The sheep shampoo quickly ran out and I had to volunteer my own, resulting in a rather highly-perfumed entry from Downe House who must, I am sure, have caused some comment among the other rams the next day. Archie was a learner flock sire, and was given a raddle harness so that we could keep track of when we might expect his lambs. One day at break, when girls could come up to the Drawing Room with anything they wished to discuss, a worried twelve-year-old came in with a problem few Heads have faced: 'Miss Farr, my ewe has blue at both ends. Do you think Archie knows what he is doing?'

The Young Farmers exhibiting at the Newbury Show

St Peter's, pictured left in the 1940s, became the Headmistress's house in 1979

The House system gave an opportunity for the girls to devise their own House Services, and a great deal of thought and well-honed execution went into these. The Upper Sixth asked to be responsible for Remembrance Sunday, giving us several deeply moving reminders of the tragedy of war. The annual Confirmation Service developed from being a hideously embarrassing fashion show (the recollection of my first at Downe is still searing) to a very beautiful annual service in St Nicolas Church, Newbury. Many girls were confirmed by Eric Wilde, Bishop of Reading, who had

a marvellous sense of humour and was just the right person to challenge any teenager indulging in woolly thinking. If he took Evensong for us, he would wait until we reached 'the rich He will send empty away' in the Magnificat and then transmit a large wink in my direction across the chancel.

By then Choral had grown in size, but places were prized as highly as ever. A good deal of choral training had already been accomplished in the newly-formed Middle School Choir under the energetic leadership of Rosemary Kimmins. Choral, well-equipped to carry on a fine tradition of music-making, had been given lovely scarlet cassocks, firstly by the Governors and then, as it grew, by the Seniors' Association. Now, under the tutelage of Trevor Selby, a Carol Service of Nine Lessons and Carols was instituted, giving us a magnificent celebration to finish the Michaelmas term each year. It was an occasion for the whole school and parents too: quite an ordeal for the first reader, a member of the Junior School, to go up to the lectern and read to a multitude, but the assurance never wavered. Downe was learning to put on a great occasion with dignity and grace. Choral visits to cathedrals to sing Evensong became a regular part of the calendar, and whenever I could I went with them. I can never forget the pride with which I listened to their confident but ethereal sound as it rose to the lantern from the choir stalls at Ely. In my own cathedral at Hereford, Choirmaster Roy Massey, who had vowed never to have girls in the Cathedral Choir, came in during rehearsal and mistook Choral for a boys' choir: a somewhat backhanded compliment perhaps, but his praise was not easily won. Choral looked so impressive in their cassocks that they rather overshadowed the Seniors, so before long their position of responsibility was acknowledged by the introduction of green gowns.

The art department had been strong when I first arrived, and we nurtured not only those heading for Foundation courses but a healthy number of girls who chose art as a fourth A-level in place of General Studies. Walking in the footsteps of Bridget Riley from another era, we had a number who made their names in the English art scene, and on two recent occasions while staying in London I have found myself in a gallery which was hosting an exhibition from a Downe House Senior. Art history was introduced into a widening A-level programme and in Paul Risoe's care was popular, though by no means the easy option hoped for by some!

Another high point was the arrival at long last of a Careers Room and a member of staff, Jill Trumble, to watch over it and to encourage independent exploration of the many exciting prospects opening up for girls. Back in the Drawing Room, when girls were coming to tell me of their A-level choices, more were considering newly introduced subjects such as economics, while fewer science candidates needed to be discouraged from choosing English as their third subject because they couldn't live without Jennifer Gosse's inspired teaching, thereby ensuring that few if any universities would consider them with such an odd combination. They accepted the loss as a sad necessity.

Books, or the lack of them, always seemed to play a prominent part in the early days. The Library received many generous presents, the Barn Library came into being as a Middle School fiction and junior reference library, and the Book Shop was created by the English department. A good many staff proved that they had hidden talents by helping out with some superb House and school plays. I particularly remember a very successful production of Benjamin Britten's *Noye's Fludde* performed in St Nicolas Church, when virtually the whole of the middle and lower part of the school metamorphosed into animals and birds in some magnificent costumes created by the art department.

Jennifer Kingsland, impressive in her own WRNS uniform, took an intrepid band to form the first WRNS contingent of the CCF at Bradfield. I couldn't believe that they had taken to

David Fox was a truly memorable economics teacher. The class all seemed just to gell, and though he worked us hard, nothing was dry and boring and we loved our lessons. However, what made him special was that he made a fantastic effort for us. As part of his mission to improve our all-round education he decided that we should go to the filming of *Question Time* and wrote to the BBC for tickets. They wrote back to say they didn't allow schoolchildren, whereupon he wrote again informing them that we were not schoolchildren but 'mature Sixth Form students'. The tickets duly arrived, and when we got there three of us were chosen to ask questions! What doubled the pleasure was seeing the look on Mr Fox's face. I well remember the train ride home – Mr Fox in a railway carriage with ten 'mature Sixth Form students', all of us bursting with pride.

Sarah Lang (Carter, 1987)

117

black lisle stockings and black lace-up shoes so readily. Even hiking and camping on the very wet Brecon Beacons were taken in good spirit, and I remember driving to a celebration CCF dinner under canvas to join the Bradfield Headmaster for a very acceptable meal produced in appalling conditions. Bradfield, our nearest boys' boarding school, was good to us as we gathered momentum. We accepted eagerly an invitation to provide actors for their remarkable Greek plays, and in *Antigone* we found for them the only Sixth Former on the stage who was actually studying A-level Greek and could therefore read from the script in rehearsal. Charles Lepper had by that time forgiven me for allowing so many girls to commandeer university places to read English which had been specifically earmarked for his boys!

Denis Silk, Warden of Radley, was another kind supporter. Radley were always welcome at our school dances and at House dinner parties, organised and cooked by our Lower Sixth. The boys were fun, but trustworthy and considerate too and a great tribute to their own school. Denis was always prepared to ease our path where he could. I remember him ringing one Saturday morning when a party of Radley boys was due in the evening. 'I have just had a look at the list of boys coming to Downe, and some young gentlemen on it wouldn't have been my first choice. . . . I think I shall come.' How many Arnolds or Roxbrughs would have made a similar gesture on a Saturday evening? It was a humbling lesson.

As Downe House approached the point when its size had doubled, we were faced by a new and unwelcome threat as many of the boys' public schools began to find keeping boys on into the Sixth Form more difficult. As a newly-regenerated school we were obvious prey. We were still regarded by some who didn't know the recent story as not in the first rank of girls' independent schools, and I was still spending time with every prospective new parent selling the recent changes. Our own girls were easily lured, for most girls at sixteen are ready for a change and few realise the extreme disadvantage this can prove to be if the boys' school chosen has an ethos entirely centred on provision for the boys. Nor did they reckon on the precious Sixth Form time wasted while they became acclimatised to a new school and new teachers.

I personally found fighting grimly to retain our girls, sometimes in the face of fathers determined that their daughters should finish their education in the Neo-Gothic edifices of their own school-days, an enervating and time-filling occupation which I resented greatly when there was so much still to do at Downe. I have always believed that true coeducation, from the start and with teachers carefully trained to understand gender differences, should be an option for parents, but this calculating and arrogant rape of the girls' schools was and is a disgraceful chapter in the recent history of the minor boys' public schools.

By now the weakness in science teaching and public examination results at Downe had been repaired. Susan Colebrook had turned the chemistry department around, and we had acquired other excellent new staff, Bob White to head the biology department and Diane Rogers, followed by Tom Packer, to lead the physics staff. Bob had resigned from leading his large department at Burford School, one of the foremost comprehensive schools in the country, because Oxford Education Authority insisted that the lower streams were to be taught environmental science, when Bob had already experienced proven success with them in the GCSE biology syllabus. Such can be the idiocy of LEAs. He was a huge gain to our science department, and was perhaps the only person who could have in any way replaced Margaret Gill, our former Head of Biology, who had died suddenly while still in her thirties, leaving her husband with two small children to bring up. She was full of enthusiasm and warmth as well as a skilled teacher; her loss was a bitter blow to everyone at Downe.

After the newcomers were settled, we seemed poised to launch into another round of building in order to give them much needed room in a new Science School, and room for Information Technology too. As always, funds were hard to find and we had no more small houses to sell off in Cold Ash. Miss Willis seemed to have had an eye for property investment, but even she couldn't have foretold the enormous leap in property values as Cold Ash became a commuter village, nor how her small property acquisitions would prove so much to our benefit financially. It was as I was about to depart that the plans were agreed and the site manager for the Science School was appointed. In many ways I wished that I could have been there to watch it grow from the window by my desk.

The first eight of my eleven years at Downe had been utterly exhausting and all-involving, and although we were now beginning to settle to happier times, and a much larger school, the administrative burden grew and I found myself spending less and less time with the girls. Easy relationships with pupils had in my past been such an enjoyable aspect of professional life, but I now realised that, in creating a much larger school, I had irrevocably distanced myself from teaching and from the girls themselves. I had superb support from my Senior Mistress, Dorothy Goode, and from Alison Gwatkin

**Senior staff in 1989:
left to right, Mrs Goode,
Miss Farr, Mrs Gwatkin,
and Mrs Moore**

as Senior Housemistress, who was to prove so vital to Downe's future in heading up a first-rate team of House staff and again at a later stage in the interregnum. But even with these highly skilled organisers at my side, I began to feel that between us we had laid sufficient foundations for a secure future for the school and that it was time for fresh eyes to oversee the next chapter before once again complacency and self-congratulation could set in. There were a host of experienced staff capable of ensuring that recent achievements could be consolidated to become firm, unshakable foundations for the future.

On a personal front, after twenty-six years in boarding schools, I yearned for a life at home, some roots in Herefordshire, and the normal life which headmistresses rarely enjoy. No school would, or could, ever replace the affection I felt for Downe House, or rival the golden girls who had come through to the top during my time. We had tried in every way possible to give them the normal atmosphere, so espoused by the Founder, in which to grow up, as well as a rich array of opportunities to set them on their way in a modern world. It was time for me to move on.

Science and other academic development

Preparation of hydrogen
sulphuric acid or zinc
$H_2SO_4 + Zn = ZnSO_4 + H_2$

BELOW: **Darwin's laboratory in Kent**

Throughout its existence Downe House has maintained a high reputation for the teaching of the traditional arts subjects – mainly English, history, the classics, and modern languages. But for the first fifty years, the sciences were less well served. Much of this was due to attitudes prevailing at the time; before the Second World War, most girls' schools included nature study and some botany on the curriculum, but chemistry was limited to basics and the study of physics a rarity. Qualified female science teachers formed a select and rather odd breed. Downe was fortunate – and somewhat unusual – in having excellent and dedicated science teachers

OPPOSITE AND ABOVE:
The laboratory at Cold Ash in the 1920s

RIGHT: **The Chemistry laboratory in 1934**

in Miss Heather and, later, Miss Rippon. But, as pupils of the time recall, there was not a great deal of emphasis placed on what were then regarded as the more esoteric subjects. Judith Hubback (Williams, 1934) writes: 'The library was very well stocked. Any of us who wanted to could get up early (ie 6.30am) and work there, happily unsupervised, before morning Chapel and breakfast. . . . History under Jean Rowntree, Latin under Miss Smith, and English under Mamie Poore were very well taught indeed. . . . Science in all forms was more or less pathetic . . . '.

Mary Midgley (Scrutton, 1937), the distinguished philosopher, recalls, in her memoir *The Owl of Minerva,* her experience of the academic standards at Downe in her time. 'Geography was

– as it is in many places – a vacuum, of which I remember only the oxbow lake. Botany I quite liked, but it dealt only with classifying plants. Physics and chemistry struck me at first as rather exciting when I began to hear about heat and light and the chemical elements. But I soon discovered that what really mattered in science was simply to produce neat and elegant homework, all in the passive voice, with the apparatus tidily drawn through a stencil and absolutely no blots. As for mathematics at Downe, I was quite willing to be interested, but the lady who taught us did not make it very clear and she usually preferred to talk about something else. The class encouraged this habit, laying bets as to how soon she could be got off the subject onto some other topic, such as drains.

'Our French teaching was educational in a different way. We had a cross and slightly dotty traditional Mademoiselle, clothed in shabby black dresses, who could be heard muttering curses and complaints all the time as she pottered about the school. Though some of her lessons were probably rather a waste of time, we did get used to speaking and hearing French. History (and English), however, were really well taught. Our teachers constantly brought together the many different aspects of life that history tells of, and they also connected the past with what was happening in our own day. One of them, Jean Rowntree, used to give a fortnightly talk to the whole school about current events, which at the time included important matters like the rise of Nazism. She made it all live, yet she always made some sense of it. She also reached back often into the past to show how the strange things that seemed to be happening now could have become possible – what people had meant by acting in this way, what states of mind had shaped our world.'

Patience Thomson (Bragg, 1952) records: 'A tremendous highlight was being allowed to substitute "Plato" for lacrosse. We had our

122

sessions with a retired headmaster who treated us like adults and we responded accordingly. "Define the soul, Patience," he would say. There was a roaring fire in winter and a revolving summerhouse in the summer. I also had a brilliant teacher of German who spoke little English and had been in the Polish resistance during the war. She taught me how to blow up a train and the joys of Goethe's poetry. English was imaginatively and skilfully taught by Miss Barnsley, who seemed to have endless time for us. We lay on the grass outside her house on summer Sunday afternoons, eating cake and discussing poetry.'

After the move to Cold Ash, science took a step forward with the building in 1923 of the Science Laboratory, housed in the new buildings erected beyond the Cathedral Steps. Miss Heather continued to teach, but she was also Olive Willis's Deputy, so school administration took up increasing amounts of her time. It was the arrival of Miss Rippon in 1928 which started the long, slow progress to improve matters. She was both an innovative and inspirational teacher, but she also had to fight a continual battle against inadequate accommodation, equipment, and time. She maintained her struggle until her retirement in the 1960s, but she left firm foundations for the future.

Slowly the allocation of time increased, although two single lessons per week to cover all three sciences were still considered adequate until the 1950s. Eve Miller (Latham, 1963) was one of the few pupils studying the sciences at Downe in the 1950s and 1960s, unusually for the time strongly encouraged by her mother: 'As was so often the case for women born in 1912, my mother lived all her life regretting her lack of formal education and so, just to prove she could, shock/horror she went off and did her nursing training at fifty years of age. Against this background she was determined that this daughter should have a proper formal education

The school's first computer in the 1980s

in general, and in maths and science in particular. It was lucky that I enjoyed the potential dramas of the chemistry lab rather than those provided by Shakespeare and, along with a couple of other fifteen-year-olds (including Elizabeth Nowell-Smith who went on to do pure maths and on that basis was thought to be very odd!), proceeded from general science O-level to physics, chemistry, and maths for science at A-level.

'I have many memories, including spending a lot of time diverting comments that I must be a bluestocking. I didn't know what the phrase meant but at that age one is desperate to fit in and I guessed it was less than complimentary. At school I was large and clumsy and struggled with doing microanalysis, and I spent the physics lessons rewriting the syllabus to include repairing irons and other domestic appliances to fit us for the "housewife" role we all expected to fill. One repaired things then. Science Club met only intermittently because there were so few of us.

'There was little career advice, but I was absolutely determined not to be a deb even if it condemned me to a life of spinsterhood. My mother, despairing that I would ever make it socially because I refused to abandon my glasses, said I would have to get a job and duly filled in the application forms to the thirteen Medical Schools then in existence in the UK and Ireland. She also investigated Melbourne University in case Charing Cross Hospital changed their policy on this token girl at the last minute. I thank my mother, father, and science teachers at Downe on a daily basis for enabling me to have a really fascinating career and – oh yes – a thirty-four-year marriage.'

By 1964, growing realisation of the importance of science for girls, long established in the girls' grammar and high schools, had finally reached Downe. The Headmistress, Mrs Bourdillon, oversaw the planning of a new

The Chemistry laboratory in 1985, above, and the Physics laboratory in 1980, left

Science Block, which was opened by Dorothy Hodgkin in 1967. It contained four laboratories, a preparation room, and a dark room. Ten years later there were five staff, led by Evelyn White, but no technician, and girls taking sciences in the Sixth Form continued to be a minority.

With the arrival of Miss Farr in 1978, the emphasis on science increased. Additional experienced staff were appointed, and the first qualified technician employed, succeeding a 'washer-up' seconded from the kitchen. Downe had missed out on the heavy promotion of

124

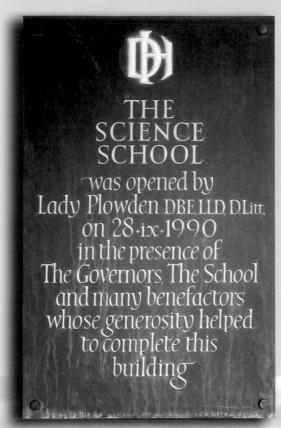

THE
SCIENCE
SCHOOL
was opened by
Lady Plowden DBE, LLD, D.Litt,
on 28·ix·1990
in the presence of
The Governors, The School
and many benefactors
whose generosity helped
to complete this
building

The new Science School, opened by Lady Plowden in 1990

science in the 1960s, when industry gave open-handedly to schools in order to obtain able scientists in the future, so although the laboratories were well equipped, there were too few, making timetabling impossible. Upper Sixth physicists will no doubt recall learning electronics in Room R which contained one rather erratic power point.

Miss Farr was determined that more laboratories should be built and, once even more pressing priorities had been met, a fresh appeal was launched. The new Science School was opened by Lady Plowden in 1990, and since then the science department has played a major role in school life. All girls now take all three sciences at GCSE and many continue in the Sixth Form. Many girls read science-related subjects at

Chemistry lesson
in 2000

university, and they succeed too in national competitions including science essays, Olympiads, and much-sought-after places on Sixth Form engineering courses.

Many of the staff are well established, and the ensuing stability and quality of teaching has greatly contributed to the increasing numbers and success of those studying the sciences. Among these are Joanna Wood, Jennifer Kingsland, Ian Watson (famed especially for his pyrotechnic expertise), Sue Foote, Rosanna Oldham, Ohmar Spence, and Debbie Hicks, and

a team of qualified technicians, led by Sue Brown. A Science Society for the older girls, which invites eminent scientists to speak on a wide variety of scientific disciplines, together with a more practical Science Club for the younger ones, have ensured that breadth of experience as well as detailed knowledge have continued to flourish. The changing fortunes were recognised by the inspection report of 1999, which commented on 'the very strong, well qualified team of teachers and technicians working with enthusiastic, highly motivated girls.'

CHAPTER 5
Other perspectives

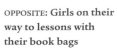

OPPOSITE: **Girls on their way to lessons with their book bags**

Academic life 1979–2004

Jack Bayliss

A very early encounter saw a girl asking me if I had come from Wycombe Abbey. When I said that I had come from a school in Wales, she asked what I was doing at Downe House. Thinking quickly, I replied that I was on missionary work.

In those early days I did indeed feel like David

Jack Bayliss

Livingstone, trekking through unknown territory in the hope of converting the natives. There is no doubt that there were many talented and friendly pupils, but extracurricular activities were, to many, seemingly more important than academic achievement and relatively few stayed on in the Sixth Form. Had league tables existed in those days, one would have had to go a long way down the list to see Downe House mentioned.

It would have been easy to seek new pastures, but I was determined to play a part in raising academic standards. It was most fortunate for us that Suzanne Farr had been appointed as Headmistress. The decisions and actions which she took were not always popular, but popularity was not her aim; she preferred to set her sights on making Downe House an admirable school where standards in all areas would be the highest. In 1989, Baroness Warnock wrote the following appreciation of Miss Farr on her retirement as Headmistress: 'She demanded excellence; and increasingly in her time, we, the Governors, simply have begun to take it for granted that that is what we have got: excellence in academic achievement, in the arts, in games, in manners, in the ethos of the school. To achieve this, Miss Farr has brought together a team of people on the staff who share her vision, and whose work has become more and more distinguished.'

In 1981 York House was opened for members of the Upper Sixth. I was appointed as Housemaster,

and I am indebted to the support which my wife gave me during the next five years in the House. There were twenty 'inmates', as the girls referred to themselves. This is small by today's numbers but herein lay the seeds of the future success of Downe House. By 1989 there were two Upper Sixth Houses and today there are four Sixth Form Houses. The establishment of these Houses has played an important part in the raising of academic standards.

The improvement in academic achievements in the period 1979–2004 has been remarkable. When Miss Farr left Downe House in 1989 the number of students in the Sixth Form had grown considerably. Miss Cameron's inheritance was a school which was well on its way to becoming one of the premier educational establishments in the country. In November 1994 the *Daily Telegraph* published a league table of A-level results. Downe House was the top girls' boarding school. The *Financial Times* also produced an analysis of the A-level performance of all independent schools and Downe was in eighth place. Today we take it for granted that, in any national survey of examination results, Downe House will be in a prominent position.

In my early years at Downe few girls went on to Oxford or Cambridge, but after 1990 the number of Sixth Formers achieving places at these universities increased dramatically. There are few colleges at either that have not seen Downe students passing through their portals. But there has also been a significant expansion in the range of other universities at which girls have gone on to study. This is, in no small measure, due to the excellent Careers department which was started by Mrs Trumble and then developed by Mrs Oldham.

These years have seen a broadening of the curriculum to create much more variety in the range of subjects available for pupils to study, including politics, economics, classical civilisation, theatre studies, sports science, computer studies, business studies, and Russian. Miss Cameron's introduc-

tion of the French Project, which involved members of the Lower Fourth spending a term in France, added a new dimension to the Downe House educational experience.

When I left Downe in 2004 I was able to observe a highly successful school but I reminded

Miss Cameron

myself that it is easy to admire a beautiful garden and yet forget the hard work that has made it what it is. The present reputation of the school owes much to the contributions made by many people over the past twenty-five years. Like ardent gardeners they planted the seeds and nurtured the plants.

I remember a wise Cambridge don saying to me that the achievement of excellence was much easier than maintaining it. I have no doubt that Downe House will not fail to maintain and further its present reputation.

Jack Bayliss came to Downe in 1979 as Head of history and Housemaster of Holcombe House. He became Housemaster of York House in 1981 and Director of Studies in 1989, a post he held until he retired in 2004.

131

OPPOSITE: **The library in 1990 with portrait of Olive Willis**

The evolution of boarding
Alison Gwatkin

The inception of the House system, shortly after Suzanne Farr's arrival, caused a great upheaval in the life of a boarder at Downe. Talking to Old Seniors who lived through this period is interesting! For them, the pastoral cohesion this brought spelled out loss of freedom and loss of friendships, and was a cause of much debate. But Miss Farr's vision prevailed. House spirit grew, but at the same time Downe has never lost the sense that the House structure serves the community as a whole. Girls at Downe have grown to love their House identity – reinforced now with hoodies, logos, mugs, and all the paraphernalia of a special 'brand'. Yet away from the competitive arena the girls still experience a feeling of belonging to the whole community, actively supporting their year group and all the other years in the House.

From the early 1980s the tightness of the boarding structure served Downe well. Under the

York House when new

132

inspirational leadership of Lynne Berwick, girls who entered the school at eleven were given a secure foundation. They lived in Houses separate from the main school, learning to board first of all. Guided from morn till dusk, they were taught the routine and that excellence was the watchword in all areas: work, standards of behaviour, dress, or packing a book bag! The girls found their feet quickly, and secure on that foundation they were released to develop a whole range of hitherto untapped skills.

From the mid-1980s Mary Moore took up the mantle. Her vision and compassion, combined with adherence to the routine punctuated with amazing surprises, soon cast her as a legend. Tough, elegant, and funny all at once, she inspired the girls to achieve their best.

The Sixth Form soon began to chart a successful track record of academic results, which continues to this day. Jack Bayliss – later a most distinguished Director of Studies – opened the newly appointed York House for the Upper Sixth as the first major phase of building in Miss Farr's time got underway. The newly appointed Senior Housemistress ran the first leadership course for Sixth Formers in 1987, and the outstanding leadership offered by the dedicated team of well-qualified teaching House staff – who led in the Staff Common Room as much as in the House! – consolidated this strong base. At Staff Meetings, when the appointment of Seniors was being discussed or the choice of GCSE subjects for the Upper Fourth, each Housemistress in turn would speak for her girls one by one until the Headmistress was satisfied that the right decisions had been made.

Being known and being cared for have always been central to the pastoral vision at Downe. At this time only the Upper Sixth lived separately at York House, and twelve- to seventeen-year-olds were catered for in mixed-age Houses. The sense of community within these Houses was enormous, encompassing as they did most of a girl's life in school. Sport, Drama, and Music were the most

133

A birthday party

hotly contested competitions and gave the older girls a real taste of leadership. Charity events were soon added to the portfolio and the Houses, under the leadership of Sixth Form girls, showed great enterprise in raising large sums of money for charities all over the world.

Early in the 1990s, as the numbers continued to rise, Miss Cameron sought to expand the boarding experience of the girls by setting up what has come to be known as the French Project. All the girls in the Lower Fourth would spend one term in France, in order to broaden cultural horizons, create a focus far beyond just speaking in French, and help to build on all they had learnt in the first year about living in a community. At about the same time, work was started on a long overdue Sixth Form House, over by the pines and across the way from the now bulging York House. Originally planned as a Lower Sixth House, it was very quickly realised that we would have to pool all our resources in order to house the ever burgeoning numbers of girls flowing through the top of the school, encouraged by a broad curriculum with many added extras and a growing profile of excellent examination results.

We now refer to the Three Steps in the boarding pattern created by all these changes. This pattern is so familiar, and seems to have been achieved with such ease, that it is hard to remember the process by which we arrived here. However, this Three Step pattern has come to be a 'usp' – in modern marketing jargon a 'unique selling point' – of which the basis is that we are able to provide the appropriate level of pastoral care to each girl according to her age and level of maturity. The younger girls gain from learning to board together and developing their skills in the French Project – Step One – before entering the mixed-age Houses in Step Two, greeting in the process the ever-increasing number of girls choosing to board at thirteen-plus. Finally, the change of lifestyle offered by the Sixth Form has seen a steady increase in the number of girls staying on into that last Step Three. The three stages in school life embodied in these principles effectively offer three schools on the same campus. Always looking forward to the next stage while maintaining the same friendship groups has become a key component of life at Downe.

A crucial extra ingredient in this development has been increased involvement with parents. Listening to their concerns is key, in order to meet individual needs and to overcome obstacles to effective learning. We now as a matter of course invite parents to House dinners and charity events, so that there is a transparent understanding of how school systems work and so that we are there to answer all questions, however small. This is labour-intensive, but pays rich dividends in terms of the positive feelings promoted among parents that boarding works best when the whole family is included. The Houses seek to include new parents in the welcome package to newcomers, thus offering a real sense of community. Olive Willis's ideal, that everyone should buy into the ethos, has been truly respected, as parents, pupils, and staff

draw ever closer together to realise common goals. Knowing every girl and her parents has always been a priority for the present Headmistress, Emma McKendrick. Her commitment to this ideal, and the personal touch that makes all the difference to life at Downe, is exemplified in the birthday card she sends to each girl.

Parents support the girls and staff in many ways, not just at parents' meetings and house events but also on games and music tours. Memories of Venice and Rome will always linger as precious moments when education in its widest sense was being delivered to all. In parallel, Downe puts great emphasis on its active tutorial work, and was complimented for this in our recent inspection. Data and statistics have their importance; but one-to-one communication still makes that unquantifiable difference that is the basis of success. Over the last ten years Downe has worked in successful partnership with parents to support needy girls experiencing the tough, life-changing challenges of adolescence. Seeing them emerge triumphant at the end has been most satisfying.

As others fell by the wayside, Downe stuck to its guns as a full boarding school offering excellent 24/7 care and an enviable weekend activity programme supported by highly committed staff. Abseiling for newcomers creates a bonding weekend, alongside cultural trips, cinema evenings, and makeover days – not to mention socials, debates, and plays with Radley. The girls have considerable input into this programme, and are also increasingly involved in the running of the school through their involvement in committees and councils and through the Leadership Challenge offered to all Sixth Formers so that they may understand how the school ethos is delivered in practice. The next hundred years will produce its share of challenges. However, to see so many exciting initiatives for the future already in place is encouraging, and reinforces the ethos of the school that has prevailed for the whole of its first hundred years. We still expect our leavers to feel

**Junior Choral at
St Peter's in Rome**

the same as one clearly did; as she eloquently put
it: 'I left Downe House with the feeling that there
was nothing I could not achieve.'

*Alison Gwatkin was appointed as Housemistress of Tedworth
in 1985 and a year later became Senior Housemistress. She
combined both roles until 1996 when she was appointed
Acting Headmistress for a year. Since 1997 she has been
Deputy Headmistress.*

The Junior School

Mary Moore

When I took over the running of the Junior School, I was helped by the fact that the highest standards had already been well established by Lynne Berwick, with whom I worked in tandem for the first term.

I also had three guiding principles of my own: to provide stability, to remain objective, and to love the girls in my care. I also needed a sense of humour. The little girls in my care had often not been away from home before and both they and their parents needed to feel secure; I could not afford to be wishy-washy.

This sense of security was aided by a strong, and basically unchanging, supportive pastoral team who all followed the same guiding principles. And although the girls were divided between the two Junior Houses which were mildly competitive, we all ate, worked, and played together. This continuity of staff and ideals provided a sense of home, for this is what a successful House had to

Removes outside Hill House

Removes at Hermitage House

be for that all-important first year. I also taught all the first-year girls and this provided me with an all-encompassing awareness of their development in every area of their lives. During this first year the girls had to grow up, learn independence, and feel ready to face the demands of the main school. In these early years, the girls all went into a mixed-age House at the end of their first year – it is only latterly that they have spent their second year in the upper Junior School House. Our task, therefore, was to develop each girl's potential so that she was confident to move on. This imperative still continued when we faced the challenge of managing the change and excitement of a term in France during the girls' second year.

Physically the Junior School structure has changed too, in that the Houses have retained their names but moved to other buildings. The first Junior House was in Hill House, built for Miss Willis's retirement and where Miss Farr had

lived. The second Junior House, Darwin, was developed from the old school Sanatorium at the top of the drive, and so both Houses were physically removed from the main school. In 1996, as the numbers continued to increase, I moved off-site to the village into Hermitage House, which

138

housed all the first years for the Remove year. It was then decided to have a Lower Fourth House so that the girls who were spending a term in France were given a more cohesive second year together. Now the Junior Houses retain the original House names but – apart from Hermitage – are not in the original buildings.

During my years in charge there were many changes and, back in 1984 when I started, life was tougher than it is today; but once the girls and their parents realised that they were in secure hands, a happy, relaxed atmosphere soon prevailed and I watched the girls' developing independence with pride. It seems extraordinary now to think that girls and parents survived with only two exeats and a picnic each term (often, it seemed, in the pouring rain in a steamed-up car) in which to meet, apart from special events such as concerts and sporting events. There were at that time no mobile phones or even phone calls home except on high days and birthdays, but the close-knit family we became provided a superb support

Fashion created from black bin bags

system; no problem was left unattended or unresolved. Gradually over the years things have inevitably changed, but the rule of 'Do as you would be done by' and a deep commitment to others' needs remained our cornerstone.

I have, of course, too many memories of my years to mention, but must share a few. In the early years we ate at small round tables above the Dining Room in what is now a computer/study area. There was waitress service and formal table manners were *de rigueur*. One of my first tasks, therefore, was to show the assembled company how to cut, peel, and eat the fresh fruit which was provided daily. Initially this caused both consternation and difficulty for some, but Old Seniors I meet to this day inform me that they still feel that they are letting the school down when they eat fruit any other way.

Cloaks symbolised winter, and when we went on our annual trip to the British Museum they always drew the admiring attention of the public; but to me they are a crocodile going up the Woodland Path to breakfast. To the girls in their first term they were the final, mysterious excitement of the whole school Christmas Dinner when Choral, concealed in their cloaks, processed around the Dining Room and Gallery by candlelight singing carols. However, they were also very versatile garments and an integral part of our many evening activities, doubling as caves, bedspreads, and even the back end of a horse.

Plays and entertainments were always a part of Junior School life, be they ice-breakers at the beginning of the year or a chance for budding stars to show off their talents. I was always amazed at the girls' ingenuity with costume and – although black plastic sacks and silver foil always played a part – our costume cupboard grew to provide a wide variety of styles. One particular memory is a version of 'Surrey with a Fringe on Top', mimed to a record in the hall at old Hill House, the surrey's canopy being one of the fringed bedspreads the girls all had, draped from and supported by the banisters.

We even had plays on canal banks at the end of a day's cruising when we went on our optional narrow boat holiday in the first week of the summer holidays. These were happy days indeed and, ably abetted by the redoubtable Mrs Roberts, Housemistress of Darwin, we managed two boats and twenty girls in a regime of cooking, washing-up, and lock-gate opening for five glorious days. The sun always seemed to shine and our drivers were amazed by the girls' wonderful abilities to amuse and discipline themselves. One year we even had a butty, nick-named 'The Rag-Bag', to accommodate the overflow, and this was towed along behind one or other of the engined boats. That year we were twenty-eight and our July 4th celebration went with a swing.

The Houses were always busy with both competitions and non-competitive activities. Competitions were usually non-compulsory, but most girls took part and produced amazing artefacts for the given theme, be it a Valentine mask, a carved pumpkin, an Easter bonnet, or a garden on a plate. A popular weekend activity was cookery, particularly as the participants had first pick of the results. We had to make easy things that did not involve equipment such as mixers or even scales, but the results were nearly always delicious. Jams and marmalade too provided good presents for Mummy or Granny. All these things help to bind a House together, as does the celebration of birthdays which, to a girl away from home for the first time, can prove to be an unhappy occasion. This is avoided by the much-

loved tradition of a Wacky-B full of gifts, a special cake and entertainment, and, of course, always that all-important phone call home. Each House provided its own variation on this theme, but the girl's happiness and sense of being special on that day was the vital underlying factor.

An important feature of the first year was the adventure week spent at a centre in Hampshire. This enabled all the girls to sleep and work in different groups, and meant that the day girls had a taste of boarding if they had not already had a weekend sleep-over. This became particularly important when they were all faced with spending a term in France. The adventure week had originally been instituted as a way of enabling the girls to get to know each other, out of context, before they were all split up into the mixed-age Houses. They slept in spartan conditions, which they saw as part of the challenge, but were comforted by the continuity of House Surgery and a familiar bedtime routine. The staff, too, were challenged, and I can honestly say that I did not expect to climb a rock face or abseil for the first time in my fifties! The girls made new friendships and were wonderfully encouraging and supportive of each other; moreover, no one teased anyone who opted out, though this was rare. The delight and pride on the face of a girl who had faced her fears were recognised in the cheers of her friends.

Preparation for Christmas, despite the tiredness engendered by the length of the term and the newness of everything for the girls, was always an exciting time, but for me the Junior Nativity Play was special. We tackled demanding plays written by authors such as John Arden and Seamus Heaney, and the girls, as always, rose admirably to the challenge. Parts were learned over the Long Exeat, and in the final week of term the choir stalls were moved from Chapel and serious rehearsals began. The Barn Library became our dressing room reached, much to the girls' delight, by the 'secret passage' behind the Cloisters. Costumes were kept from year to year,

augmented as and when the need arose and stored in a special area of the Drama Wardrobe, originally overseen by the 'sewing ladies' on the Gallery. Our dress rehearsal was a performance in the Old People's Home in Thatcham, and parents came on the last morning of term, before the Junior School Carol Service in Jubilee Hall. As the Junior School grew, and demands on time changed, it became increasingly difficult to find a play with enough parts: a production can clearly only have so many animals and angels, and everyone had to have a walk-on part. At this point, the Music Department, in the form of Rosemary Evans, took over, with my involvement being only the final stage direction, and the results were the beautiful mini Christmas Operas, taking the place of the plays with carols. When this was over, the Junior Carol Service, with its eclectic readings, its angelic singing, and the candle-lit procession, was the essence of it all: work hard together, be disciplined, enjoy life, and support one another.

To end, I must pass on one funny story. I always had an open door policy for the Junior School – at home children are not shut out and they would not be excluded here. The girls all understood that my flat was private, but a knock on the door if I was out of sight soon brought me into view, night or day. One little sister, who later joined the House, did not know this unspoken rule and came looking for me. I was on the loo, door open of course, and there she found me. She was quite unconcerned (I felt I had to be the same!) and we had a long conversation until she heard Mummy calling. Released, I sorted myself out and went to find Mummy, telling her of the situation and laughing about it. Mercifully, when this little girl was bigger and joined the House, she had forgotten about this incident and I forbore to remind her. But, though my doors remained open, such an episode was not repeated!

Mary Moore was Head of the Junior School from 1984 to 2001.

Painting and singing at Downe
Paul Risoe

Life has taught me that two of its greatest experiences come from the enjoyment of painting and singing, so it was my good fortune that I could indulge in such pleasures during my time at Downe. All of us who worked in the old Art Room remember it with affection. On my first, memorable visit I was struck by the number of easels. At the other schools where I had taught art the easel was an endangered species. Here there was a veritable forest of them – almost as if the pine trees had followed me up the stairs and taken on a beautiful metamorphosis.

What is so special about the easel? It forces the student to confront the making of a painting, whether the work is from the imagination or from direct observation. The analogy of this confrontation with that of the singer taking on an audience is an attractive one. Both painter and singer can see the shaping of their creation, and both acts can take on the physical nature of a dance. I know that art is not taught to produce artists, but in that lovely Art Room all became artists.

I can pick out only some personalities. One morning in the early 1980s I was told, in a rather

The Art Room in 1987

The Pottery Studio in 1987, below, and the Art Room in the 1930s, bottom

disapproving manner, that the lights in the Art Room had been left on late into the night. The reason for this misdemeanour was Katrina Verdon-Roe emulating her hero, Edvard Munch, with a life-size nude self-portrait. After her interview at the Slade she received a most complimentary letter from the late Lawrence Gowing (I hope she still has it). The lesson that stays most in my memory was one where the Sixth Form had arranged their own session. Two of them, provocatively posed in dramatic lighting and bringing together the two adversaries, Delacroix and Ingres, into complete harmony of line and colour, inspired some of the most powerful Sixth Form work I had ever seen. The artist Fiona Rae, who now enjoys a considerable international reputation, wanted to read English while at school but nevertheless made part of the Art Room her domain while working on her A-levels.

Soon after arriving at Downe I was asked by Albert Sidebottom, then Director of Music, to become involved in the production of the operas. Albert and, later, Trevor Selby were most ambitious in their repertoire, and in a decade or so they put on the likes of Mozart, Puccini, Britten, Purcell, and Humperdinck. Perhaps the most ambitious production was of Britten's *Noye's Fludde*, performed in St Nicolas Church in Newbury, in which nearly the whole school was involved. The production that gave me the greatest pleasure was Malcolm Williamson's *The Happy Prince*. Jane Haughton, later to sing at Covent Garden, was a commanding Statue, with a powerful and imposing voice, and Natalie Hatton was a most touching Match Girl.

Albert Sidebottom, Trevor Selby, and I were insistent on the singers learning to project the voice without amplification – not easy in Jubilee Hall! To encourage the singers, I took my cue from that giant of a singer, the late Bruce Boyce, who used to say, 'Imagine you can drill a hole in a wall with the voice.' I would exhort them, 'Remember that you are a violin, not a piano, and sing to the clock at the back of the hall. If you can make that clock hear and understand, the audience will.' It is all in the imagination; and how well the young singers rose to the challenge.

What is it that is so compelling and moving about such singing? The key word is 'legato',

The Barber Shop Quartet: left to right, Mr Sidebottom, Mr Bayliss, Mr Risoe, and Mr Selby

which is comparable to the convincing use of line, colour, and shape in a painting. Some had the ability and imagination to phrase, where the musical line took on a plastic quality associated with painting and sculpture. While working on Puccini's *Sister Angelica*, Mary Naismith, the Angelica, and I were discussing a difficult point of movement and music, and she suddenly said it was a little like Michelangelo. She could really hold an audience with her singing and acting, and later made a memorable Anna Leonowens in *The King and I*, the first musical which Trevor Selby put on after a decade of operas.

In the final school assembly of the summer of 2004, we long-serving old-timers were treated to Alice Whittaker singing Gershwin's 'Summertime'. To stand up in front of the whole school in the morning and sing takes some bottle. Alice has a lovely, powerful voice, but what is just as impressive is her expressive use of it. There we have it, both painting and singing remembered as powerful forms of expression.

Paul Risoe joined the school in 1975 as an art teacher, later becoming Head of art and of history of art

LEFT: **Mary Naismith in** *The King and I*

Rope and Net, by
Hannah Lord

Abstract, by
Camilla Emson

Anger, by Luella
Hitchcock

Elizabeth, by Kate Guest

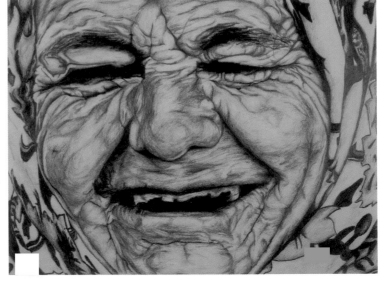

Face, by Libby
Wyman

Channelling energies
Jennifer Kingsland

Olive Willis as Guide Commissioner

145

U niformed organisations have never played a major role in school life, although Girl Guide Companies flourished for much of the first fifty years and a Girls' Training Corps was formed during the Second World War.

The Combined Cadet Force (CCF) was a fixture in most boys' schools and a few coeducational ones, but was unheard of in girls-only establishments. However, in 1984, the option of joining the Bradfield College CCF was offered to Lower Sixth girls from Downe, and to general surprise it became very popular. Girls who spent much time 'individualising' the school uniform accepted without demur the wearing of highly polished, lace-up shoes, A-line skirts of unfashionable length, unflattering berets, and acrylic jumpers. They scraped back their hair, removed jewellery, and submitted enthusiastically to military discipline at Bradfield, Naval Bases, training camps, and even an Army camp in Hong Kong. Rather to the chagrin of the more experienced boys, the girls not only excelled in the more cerebral aspects of the training (chartwork, navigation, strategy, and tactics), but also quickly became proficient at weaponry, shooting, drill, assault courses, night exercises, and general fieldcraft.

The greatest test for each group came with the (now defunct) forty-eight hours Arduous Training Exercise on the Brecon Beacons. Living under canvas, eating army rations, carrying all their kit, and walking and climbing in terrain used as SAS training grounds brought out impressively the good humour, fortitude, and resilience of the girls. No matter the time of year, the weather always seemed extreme on those weekends, ranging from freezing winds with

The Combined Cadet Force in 1994

driving snow or rain to relentlessly intense heat and sun.

Sadly, in recent years, increasing numbers of public examinations made coordinating the time-tables of the two schools first difficult and then impossible, and the collaboration has lapsed. However, it had a certain legacy, in that a few of those who participated while in school went on to make a career in the Services. Hatty Wells (1996) is now an Army Medical Officer, and recalls, 'one of the camp days, when we did a mock platoon attack on a hill. We had had a briefing the night before, so we thought we could handle it. We also had quite a dishy regular army instructor and it was a sunny day, so things looked pretty good. I was in the reserve section that was going to give covering fire to the assault. Forced to lie face down in a bog for about two hours, I felt a toad (ugh!) crawling up my leg, and when I tried to crawl out of the stinking water, I was told by the instructor to be quiet and get back in. He didn't seem so nice then! I had a great time being a cadet in the CCF. I did try to join the naval university cadet pro-gramme, but they had no stand at the freshers' fair so I joined the London University OTC instead. So that's why I chose to be an army doctor instead of a navy one.'

The introduction of the Duke of Edinburgh Award in the early 1980s has been a great success. Led by Denny Hooper, the take-up was initially quite small but over the years the numbers have grown. Successive organisers, especially Rosemary Morgan and Linda Smallwood, have cajoled and persuaded many staff to assist with training and assessment. The first Gold Awards were obtained in 1986, after training by the indefatigable Sue Foote. Currently most of the Lower Fifth work towards the Bronze Award and a number proceed on to the Gold. The combination of physical, mental, and community service training has proved a lasting attraction.

The fallow period at the end of the summer term, after the intense concentration by the Upper Fifth on their first public examinations, can be a challenging time for Housemistresses and other staff. Working on the premise that 'occupied girls cause less trouble', the practice of taking the whole year off-site was first adopted in the late 1970s.

CCF camp

RIGHT AND OPPOSITE:
Outward Bound

**Duke of Edinburgh
Gold expedition**

Initially the girls went camping, many for the first time in their lives, and mostly at Breinton on the Welsh border where they slept under canvas, cooked, hiked, pony-trekked, and canoed. Though these expeditions were much enjoyed by all, the organisation required each year was difficult for already busy staff and so in the mid-1980s it was decided to use the Outward Bound centre at Ullswater. This proved to be an excellent move and produced some unforeseen benefits. The girls were still occupied enjoyably but many of them gained much more from the experience. All learned to work well in teams, with many, especially the less athletic, gaining physical confidence; and in addition, the week brought out latent leadership qualities which proved very valuable as the girls moved on to the greater responsibilities of the Sixth Form.

Wider horizons and the French Project

Miss Cameron wished to bring more people from different cultures and backgrounds to Downe – both girls and 'gap staff', who joined the school for varying lengths of time. The gap girls from New Zealand and Australia quickly became a tradition. Looked after particularly by Miss Wheaton and the PE staff, they were usually direct, outgoing, energetic, absorbed, organised, and willing to turn their hands to most things. The intake of French and Spanish *assistantes* also expanded. They helped in ways other than linguistic and became stalwart members of the school, spending a lot of time particularly with the Sixth Form and the Removes, broadening their perspectives on life in the course of their duties. Then the school branched out further and welcomed visiting *assistantes* from a wide range of other countries: Hungary, China, Ecuador, Japan, Russia, and Poland, among others. The school particularly enjoyed the English Speaking Union scholars from the USA, who were all mature and positive, and made their mark and some good friends.

Pupils from abroad arrived too, notably girls from Salem, Kurt Hahn's school in Germany. Two girls from South Africa found Downe rather casual and relaxed compared with their still rather formal, deferential system. They were shocked that girls didn't flatten themselves against the wall when the Head walked by!

Over the years, an increasing number of adventurous girls decided that one-way traffic was not enough. Projects they undertook included teaching in China, improving their German with courses in that country, French exchanges in Strasbourg, an exciting Turkish

The French house at Veyrines

exchange, and expeditions to Iceland, Russia, Seville, the Gambia, the Massif Central, Morocco, Sinai, and Namibia. Choral tours gave those participating wonderful musical and cultural experiences of life beyond Downe. And, not to be outdone, the lacrosse squad convinced the staff that an overseas tour would have huge beneficial effects on their future performance, and went to Australia twice and then to America.

But Miss Cameron felt that something more radical was necessary to maintain Downe's position in the changing educational scene and to give the girls a worthwhile, forward-looking, and unique experience. An idea was germinating:

to set up a base in another country and send a small number of girls to it each term. The Lower Fourths seemed the 'right' year group, old enough to cope with the unusual experience positively and young enough so that what they gained from the experience would underpin the rest of their schooldays and beyond.

The Governors gave the go-ahead and Miss Cameron set about finding a suitable location, with the aim of being operational by September 1991. The right property proved elusive, so the venture started in Chateau des Courgès in the village of Chailland near Laval, a small country town in Mayenne. But the location was never different enough from Britain to make the project the truly French experience Miss Cameron wanted.

The search continued, until one April day she spotted a signpost to l'Ecole Hampshire in Veyrines de Domme. It was perfect: a huge barn, now a fine classroom with dormitories and bathrooms above, other classrooms, a secretarial office, a large sitting room, two dining rooms, a very big kitchen, a house for the Principal, and what was later to be a garden. Jane Box-Grainger, who had founded the school with her husband, was thinking of retiring. So here was a ready-made, officially registered, equipped, and partially staffed school. It was tucked away in a sleepy hamlet, consisting of a few houses, hens, ducks, walnut trees, cats (and later Titi, a fierce dog which had to become an item on the risk assessment!), with the Dordogne River meandering nearby. It was decided that Veyrines should be the base for 'Downe House en France'.

Staff on both sides of the Channel worked extremely hard to make the venture a success. Of course there were problems. In France a limited number of adults had to endure twenty-four-hour contact with a small number of girls without the back-up of Seniors, staff, and the huge range of activities in the main school. The minibuses had to be driven, the telephone rang

An art class at Veyrines

incessantly at first, there were no on-the-spot maintenance men, and so on. Back in England hours were spent debating whether the girls should wear uniform or not, plus a hundred and one other minor things which mostly resolved themselves with the passage of time. Mrs Moore had already had to exert all her diplomatic skills to organise the Removes into acceptable groups for transfer to the five mixed-age Houses. Now those groups had to be remixed into three new groups to go to France term by term. Consideration had to be given to orthodontic

All the girls at Veyrines keep a journal of their stay

treatments, great-aunt Flossie's ninetieth birth-day, the gerbil having babies, music examinations, sporting prowess, parents wanting to be in France for the *vendange*, to mention but a few special requests.

Veyrines is not just about improving the girls' dexterity in the French language. Rather it is the springboard for a fully French experience: real life with the bells and smells of Veyrines and its environs replacing home for a time. Inevitably there has to be an academic curriculum, adapted to the needs of each term's girls, a process that has evolved and improved term by term. The majority of lessons are conducted in French and French is spoken for much of the time. And soon after the project started, the *sortie* was born.

These *sorties* can best be described as living lessons, with the teaching/learning process often so well disguised that it is painless and the girls forget that they are working. Several times a week each group goes off-site for periods of two to three hours, and lessons might take place in a bus-shelter, a church, a chemist, by (or in) a river, in a *cabane* on a hillside, in a pottery, in

someone's house . . . the possibilities are endless. The experiences provide maximum opportunity for seeing the area, meeting people, and speaking French. Not only is this fun (and at worst makes a change from being in a classroom) but it also means that at lunchtime (again in French) girls actually have something to talk about since they do not know what their friends have done or where they have been. Conversation is real, and though lunch in French is hard work at first it becomes easier and more natural as the term progresses.

A *sortie* does not necessarily have a destination, although over the course of a term the staff try to cover the main attractions. Many girls will remember the magic of Proumeyssac (that vast underground bubble) and the thrill of the *son et lumière*. No wonder parents enjoy visiting their daughters and sharing the buzz of Sarlat market by day and the fairytale quality of its turrets and roofs by night. Crossing the Dordogne by one of its surprisingly narrow bridges is a recurring feature of the *sorties*, as is the River Ceou with its shallow, fast-flowing

water, boulders, and eddies. The end of term *soirée* has become a hugely popular tradition, usually ending with slightly competitive renditions of the National Anthem and the Marseillaise – the blood-curdling Marseillaise inevitably being the rip-roaring winner.

In the summer term of 1996, after the examinations, the Lower Sixth A-level group went out to Veyrines, the girls thinking it would be an escape to the sun, the staff planning intensive immersion in French. For the first time Veyrines welcomed back girls who had spent a term there as Lower Fourths. They reminisced and then became very enthusiastic about improving their French, following the 'only French to be spoken' rules and accepting forfeits if heard lapsing into English. They went on *sorties*, of course. They worked enthusiastically and enjoyed going into Sarlat, Domme, and other old haunts. The staff enjoyed them too, now that they had become more independent and turned into mature young people.

The term in France continues to be a unique aspect of the total Downe House experience. There were early fears that the absence of a pupil from the main school for a whole term would have a detrimental effect on her general progress, but this has been shown to be quite groundless. Visiting parents are always thrilled by the confidence with which their daughters chatter in French, order meals with great aplomb, and show them the sights with pride. After their return to school many comment on their obviously enhanced independent spirits. Perhaps the best testimonials come from the girls themselves. Few return saying they haven't enjoyed it, and their reminiscences about Veyrines and the surrounding area are very positive.

'It was all so different – specially the sounds – M Carrié trundling past each evening with his barrow of potatoes for the pig. And the piercing horn of the *boulangerie* van in the morning.'

'I have seen friends change for the better.'

'Sorties work well when we go to fun places 'cos you actually learn when you have fun and are more disposed to listen to the teacher.'

'The weekend *en famille* was a very useful and important part of the term because it builds your confidence and you learn how a normal family in this part of France lives.'

'The smell that means Veyrines is the pungent sweet smell of cows. French cows seem to smell different from English cows.'

The Lower Sixth return to Veyrines in 1998

Broadening horizons

The Michaelmas term of 1989 saw the arrival of Susan Cameron, who was to head the school for seven years. 'Spaniels lying in dappled sunlight, a room with a view, and a warm welcome' – this is how one parent described his first encounter with Miss Cameron. He went on to describe how his daughter fell in love with the dogs and the school in that order!

Miss Cameron knew what made adolescent girls tick. They knew that she would always give

Miss Cameron

them a hearing when they brought her their ideas for charity events, summer balls, socials, and parties. She listened and somehow got them to see alternatives which would please not only them but the Housemistress who was responsible for the event. Similarly, with the staff, Miss Cameron knew how to garner ideas. Suggestions were always welcome and she would often give an individual the opportunity to try out a new idea – an open-minded approach which sometimes challenged the patience of less forward-looking colleagues. She herself had a broad view of what education really was and was always willing to explore new ways of learning. The French Project is the supreme example of this. She challenged staff to move out of their comfort zone, and many an effective strategy was evolved by this means. Having inherited a highly successful school with effective systems, she showed great wisdom in leaving those systems in place, enabling the staff to be creative with them without changing them – an approach that required imagination, patience, and modesty. She once said that, in an ideal world where she could pursue her dream of creating the perfect educational formula for each girl, she would marry the highly prized structure of the best traditional, academic school with the whacky freedom of the progressive small school, where caution could sometimes be thrown to the winds. As a historian, she was deeply interested in the ethos and the evolution of the Willis dream at Downe. She sought to appoint and promote those who had empathy with it and who would, without question, put the welfare of the girls first. The following is her own account of her philosophy and approach:

'Thanks to Miss Farr's determined, energetic, and effective Headship, I inherited a popular, stable, well-disciplined, and vibrant school, full of mostly happy, talented, and well-motivated girls. Downe House was one of the top girls' boarding schools in the country. But the goal posts were being moved. Thatcher's affluent 1980s came to an end with her fall in 1990 and a period of economic uncertainty set in. In the same year league tables appeared for the first time. After a period of

156

Jennifer Gosse

From 1943 when she arrived as a small ten-year-old, admitted early to Downe House because of the war, until 1991 when she retired, Jenny Gosse was to play a huge part in the life of the school. Her time as a pupil spanned the last four years of Miss Willis's reign and the first four of Miss Medley's, and her time as a teacher, Deputy Headmistress for a while, and Head of English embraced the revolution in approach instigated by Miss Farr and taken forward by Miss Cameron; so she was truly imbued with the ethos of Downe House at all stages of its development.

She vividly remembers the early years, when they moved bedroom every term and table in the Dining Room every two days. Like everyone else who was there at the time, she recalls the freedom to explore in threes, the jaws with Miss Willis who was both kind and formidable, flying on the Giant's Stride, and the cold and the chilblains – though, as she recalls, 'Others suffered, not I, though I remember the empurpled paws of other people who mopped their hands with methylated spirits from the huge bottle that was kept in each house.' She also benefited from the wonderful English teaching of Miss Medley and Miss Barnsley, which led to an English degree at Newnham College, Cambridge, and eventually to her return to Downe in 1960 to teach English. She stayed at the school for the rest of her career.

Coming back as a teacher, she found Downe to be a very different place: it was much bigger, and there was beginning to be increased academic pressure on the girls and growing control of the curriculum and teaching practice. But she is remembered with huge affection, both from this early period and right up to her retirement, as an extraordinary teacher, someone who truly inspired her pupils with a love of language and literature which they have kept for the whole of their lives. Indeed, she was one of the most highly regarded and well loved English teachers the school ever had: Miss Farr (chapter 4) recalls having to dissuade aspiring scientists from taking English as one of their A-levels – thus jeopardising future university places – because of their keen desire to continue to benefit from her charismatic lessons.

In the tribute on her retirement in the school *Magazine*, Miss Farr wrote: 'Headmistresses, when new, tend to be wary of three types of people: old girls of the school, because they want everything of their generation preserved in a time warp; long-standing members of staff for much the same reason; and successful, senior staff who fear that change might rock their particular boat. I was filled with apprehension on my arrival at Downe to find that Miss Gosse was a distinguished

relative security and expansion in independent schools, life suddenly became "real and earnest".

The league tables required little action by us, but they were there. The dedication of the staff and the hard work of the pupils were producing representative of all three categories. How entirely wrong I was. I would have been hard put to it to have found more loyal, trusting, and enthusiastic support. Her inspired and scholarly teaching was already legendary, but her other great gift was her unquenchable enthusiasm for the achievements, large and small, of her pupils, or indeed anyone's pupils! For her, learning is a shared journey, and achieving the goal a shared excitement. Her sincere appreciation of pupils' efforts often served as a gentle reminder in the Staff Room that striving is as praiseworthy as outstanding success.'

The entire school joined together in a celebration of their teacher at the end of her final summer term. While Miss Gosse thought it was to be a 'poetry reading' and worried about the poems she should read, the girls managed to keep their frenzied preparations secret. Staff, pupils, and old girls acted, sang, or spoke their tributes, particularly a hilarious musical version of her favourite Chaucer's *Nun's Priest's Tale*. The emotion of the occasion was summed up by a distinguished former pupil, Natalie Wheen: 'The only reason I know how to read and write is because of her. Her teaching was opening a door . . . firing a mind . . . lighting a space . . . raising a curtain . . . and having done all that she didn't take over, she let you get on with it. She gave you permission to explore. The whole school fell in love with her. She was always so surprising, so original, so extraordinary; yet also quiet, unassuming, and always very powerful.'

I remember a really bad storm which occurred when we were on a morning of revision, and a few of us got isolated in Darwin. We watched gaggles of Removes being ushered up to the main school from Hill House to start lessons, looking rather like they'd be blown away with their cloaks as parachutes. Then we went about our business as usual, until we realised that the storm was not going to just pass us by, and that we were going to have to sit it out with the rest of the school in sight but quite out of reach. Work seemed out of the question with all the noise from the wind so we were thinking about what we could cook up . . . and then the power failed, spoiling our hopes of chocolate cake or pancakes. We sat anxiously watching the trees falling around us like ninepins, some splitting, some just snapping halfway up and the top appearing to jump sideways before dropping. Thankfully, the trees all missed us, the power did return, chocolate sponge was made, and the evidence was cleared away before the wind abated.

One Halloween a practical joke was planned. Someone was dressed all in black, stocking over head, and climbed out onto the roof outside the bathrooms. A system of signals was worked out for when the correct recipient of the 'scare' was in the correct bathroom. The dark figure emerged at the planned steamed-up window to appropriately terrify the people inside, and then climbed down again, thinking that the plan had been executed to perfection. However, during the time that the signals were being exchanged, the nice Upper Fifth formers had allowed two Lower Fourth girls to go into the bathroom first, so it was they who were terrified and ran in a hysterical state of undress through the whole house, screaming and having to be calmed down with repeated explanations and lots of apologies. An early but valuable lesson was learnt about planning and identifying potential pitfalls!

Joanna Hacking (1990)

158

Hair was a vital part of life at Downe House in the 1980s. Each morning, in the thirty seconds between getting up late and being in your place at breakfast, everyone spent a great deal of time and effort backcombing their hair to create a large 'beehive' effect on the top of their heads. The larger the top roll, the better . . . or if you didn't have the right sort of hair, you had the 'flick' look which involved flicking your fringe dramatically from one side to the other. It was no great surprise that the staff went on a military-style campaign to 'anchor those wisps', which meant being hounded around the school by various members of staff desperate to attach any hair that moved to your head with a large range of hideous Kirby grips.

Eleanor Argyll (Cadbury, 1991)

more and more encouraging results, which soon shot us into the premier league. We played down this factor, but it was an underlying consideration from then on: we would not have wanted to drop down in the ratings, however much we decried them as the measure of our success as a school. Things were going well, but we could not sit back; we had to reassess ourselves in the light of a volatile educational scene in which, because of the major changes taking place in society, the role of the school in helping to prepare the girls for life beyond it was increasingly difficult to define.

I was very much in tune with Olive Willis's hatred of "schooly" schools and her encouragement of individuality, eccentricity, a certain independence of mind, and spontaneity. I shared her desire that the girls should take an adult interest in world affairs and that Downe House should be free of parochialism. I therefore instituted a number of outward-looking programmes, encouraging girls and young *assistantes* from abroad to

Children's week

This started in 1990 at the instigation of two members of the Lower Sixth, Katherine Ritchie (1991) and Philippa Blowfield (Henry, 1991), with the help of Monica Williams (Catering Manageress). Social services agreed that they could invite between ten and fifteen children, who would live at the school for a week, enjoying activities both on-site and in the neighbourhood. Local companies agreed to help with admission charges, school facilities such as the cookery and art rooms were made available, sleeping arrangements were agreed, and both fellow pupils and members of staff were enlisted to help.

The event continued for several years afterwards, again usually hosted by the Lower Sixth with the help of Jenny Howard, Housemistress and later Head of the French Project. Katherine Guinness (1997) remembers

'rounders, cooking, swimming, singing, drawing, and playing cards, as well as trips to Basingstoke leisure centre for ice-skating and bowling and to a local farm for riding. Obstacle courses, gymnastic games, and a superb sports day made the week fly past, all culminating in an unforgettable party with apple bobbing and pass the parcel.'

spend time at the school and enabling our own girls to travel abroad as well. The culmination of this initiative was the establishment of the French Project at Veyrines.'

After Miss Cameron's decision to move on at the end of the 1995/6 academic year, there was a period of transition which was magnificently filled by Alison Gwatkin as Acting Headmistress during an interregnum year. As she wrote in the 1996/7 *Magazine*, 'Promoting stability and continuity through a period of transition was the principal aim of the year. It was an opportunity to draw fresh inspiration from our roots . . . and to promote a strong feeling of team between staff, pupils, parents, Old Seniors, and Governors. I believe that the achievements of the past year are reflected in the strength of that partnership.' This message underlies the other opportunity of which Mrs Gwatkin took full advantage: this was a valuable time to draw breath after the fundamental and striking changes and development which Miss Farr had overseen, and the consolidation and growth that had followed under Miss Cameron.

The highlight of the year was the celebration of Downe's ninetieth anniversary on February 24th 1997 in Westminster Abbey. The service was attended by all current pupils and staff, parents, representatives of the wider school community including administrative, domestic, and maintenance staff, many Old Seniors, former Headmistresses, and the Headmistress-elect, Emma McKendrick. It was a splendid occasion, with glorious singing by Choral, readings by many people involved with the school including Miss Willis's great-great-niece, Clare Nelthorpe, and an address by The Reverend Dr Anthony Harvey, Canon of

A miscellany of memories: while in the Removes, 'running through the dark woodland path to Hill barely breathing with fear; Mrs Moore telling us that "the whole school will rrrag you about your socks"; putting down the names of two people you wanted to be in Senior House with; big storm when a gigantic tree came crashing down missing Junior Block by inches during a Latin lesson.' Then in the years in between, 'being allowed to watch TV on Wednesday nights and weekends; dancing to *Grease*; ironing our bread to make toast; watching the clock go round on the last forty on a Saturday morning and rushing back to see if your parents were there to pick you up; being told not to sit on the hotplates when it was freezing; Miss Wheaton saying "You're MAGIC"; trying to get back early to get a good bed at the beginning of term; having to shake hands every single night with your Housemistress at a designated time.' And finally in the Sixth Form, 'the lucky few getting cars; making toffee and taking it to supper for the whole table; queuing for hours to call errant boyfriends.'

Melissa Lee, Katharine Morrissey, and Emily Worth (Knapp-Fisher, 1992)

Westminster and a former Governor of Downe House.

During that interregnum year Mrs Gwatkin had the benefit of working closely with the new Headmistress, who took up office in the Michaelmas term of 1997. Mrs McKendrick's first *Magazine* message affirmed her commitment to 'what makes Downe House so special: its purposeful, happy, and immeasurable buzz. It is created by individuals and groups working together successfully in a whole range of areas with real value being placed on the contribution of each individual; it can

O ne of my favourite memories of my time at Downe House is of walking back to AG one evening in the pitch black with my friend Holly, after a rehearsal for *Our Town*. It was the first time I'd had a main part in a play and I felt wonderful. I was doing something I loved that was nothing to do with lessons but was an outlet for my imagination and a huge boost to my confidence, and it made me feel extremely grown up. I was fifteen, but I felt like I'd arrived.

Sophie de Albuquerque (1993)

Support staff

T he strength and support of the ancillary staff were, and are, crucial to the success of Downe House and the health and happiness of the pupils. Memories abound: of Miss Willis's French housekeeper, Madame, leaning over the Dining Room gallery brandishing an unmarked undergarment in the hope of flushing out its owner; of Elsie, the gardener from the 1930s into the 1960s, always knowing whether or not it would rain when the girls wanted to sleep out under the stars and keeping the ancient rose trees in the pepper pot garden going with a frightful fish manure which smelt vile; of generations of sewing ladies, whose domain was the Gallery and who were adept at patching djibbahs and running up wonderful costumes for the school plays. Mary Young was an institution for over forty years, as gardener, vital part of the orchestra with her double bass, and bicycle supremo during the years when almost everyone at the school had a bicycle – she is remembered for riding a bike herself while steering one or two others.

Today there are matrons who look after the houses, ensuring that the girls are safe and happy and often helping with hobbies. There are administrative staff who run the offices

and the bursary, cooks and kitchen staff, women who run the laundry, maintenance men, drivers . . . and one remarkable fact about many of these stalwarts of the school is how long most of them have stayed at Downe, and how strongly they feel that they are part of the school and important to its smooth running.

Marion Mellett and Doreen Strange

Janice Webb was Domestic Bursar for eighteen years until she retired in 2000. Doreen Strange was at Downe for thirty-five years until ill health intervened, working most of that time in the laundry. Jane Holdway clocked up over twenty-three years, and retired as domestic supervisor in January 2005. Margaret Cheeseman started as catering supervisor and has now been matron at Hermitage House for seven years. Shirley Johnson is now part-time matron of Holcombe House after twenty-six years at the school. Alison Gibbs and Marion Mellett have worked there for twenty-three years and nine years respectively, and Mrs Gibbs has even longer memories of coming to the school for tea as a child when her

Madame with Betty Ilford (Cotton, 1937)

mother worked there. Several of the maintenance and ground staff have also given many years' service, especially Tony Deacon, Jim Holmes, and Wayne Mosher, who can boast over sixty years at the school between them.

Janice Webb

Pat Lockwood, who came in 1990 as a kitchen assistant and later became supervisor, remembers the transition to a cafeteria system at mealtimes. Before this, dining arrangements were formal and strict. The kitchen staff laid the tables before the girls arrived, and the teaching staff would process through the Dining Room to the High, led by the Headmistress or the presiding mistress who would say Grace. The food was taken to hot plates on individual serving tables, and then moved onto the dining tables to be served by the member of staff at each table. There was no choice, although vegetarian options were available. Plates and cutlery were collected and then the pudding was served in the same way. This formal procedure also applied up in the Gallery, where the Removes sat, being taught table matters and correct ways of eating by their Housemistresses.

John Coffee is remembered from the 1980s as a superb chef whose food was much appreciated during the years when Monica Williams was catering manageress. She too was an institution, running the kitchens to a very high standard and also involved with other activities like Children's Week;

little girls who wanted comfort found it in playing with her dogs. The kitchens are different now, however: soon after the cafeteria system was introduced an external catering company took over the business and now employs both kitchen and domestic staff. The choice of food is now much wider, with three hot meals available – meat, fish, and a vegetable dish – together with hot vegetables and an extensive salad bar, as well as hot puddings and plenty of fruit.

Laundry arrangements have changed over the years too. Old Seniors have vivid memories of weekly collections of garments for washing ('how we must have smelled,' they comment) and djibbah blouses without collars and cuffs for easy ironing. Mrs Strange remembers rows of irons in the laundry and that it took a week for clean clothes to be returned to their owners. Mrs Webb recalls being greeted with pleasure in the local Oxfam shop when she made her regular trip to hand over bags of clothes confiscated because they were lacking name-tapes.

And what they all remember is the sense of community. There is a long tradition of staff being entertained and waited on by the girls during formal teas in Miss Willis's time, and at Christmas dinners during Miss Farr's, when husbands and children were invited too. They remember Choral singing carols by candlelight, and many of them were pleased to go to the ninetieth anniversary celebration at Westminster Abbey. Those named above are only a few of the many individuals who, over the years, are and have been an irreplaceable and vital part in the smooth running of the school.

Relaxing in one of the Houses

Some memories. Being in places like Chapel or House meetings where we were meant to be silent and someone setting everyone off with the giggles. You'd be in agony, and normally someone ended up failing to hold it in and they'd let out a snort which made it even funnier. Playing in the orchestra for Ravel's Piano Concerto and being washed over with the realisation that music was beyond everything else. And having friends you loved so totally, and who are still the most important people to you, ever.

Nina Leeming (Large, 1994)

The new Performing Arts Centre

perhaps be described best as the spirit of the school.'

The school magazines for the first seven years of Mrs McKendrick's tenure are full of achievement in all the areas which flourish at Downe House: high-level academic results; great successes in an ever-widening range of sports; high-calibre dramatic and musical performances; talented pieces of art and literary work; wide-ranging school trips all over the globe. But alongside these perhaps predictable indicators of a very successful girls' school are to be found the pointers to Downe's underlying ethos: accounts of charity work; friendly encounters with staff members; awareness of issues beyond the school in the wider world. In addition, the House reports highlight cooperative activities across all years in the context of strong House loyalties, an indication of how important the House system now is to the structure of the school.

These years have also seen considerable upgrades and improvements in the physical environment, many of them funded through the generosity of parents, Governors, and friends of the school. Anyone from the early years at Cold Ash visiting now would still easily recognise the central buildings, especially the main building, the Chapel, the Cloisters, the Concert Room, the Cathedral Steps, and the Dining Room, although many of these have been altered or tidied up. But these visitors would fail to recognise a great deal else. The boarding houses have been extended to give much roomier accommodation – they might even come across as luxurious, with carpeted floors, modern showers and bathrooms, comfortable common rooms, and much more individual space. There is a magnificent new Sports Hall – the Farr Centre – with well-equipped sports facilities and also a dance studio, a fitness room, and excellent changing rooms. Jubilee Hall – now part of a grand Performing Arts Centre – has been extended and improved, with new lighting systems, an imposing entrance and large foyer, and excellent facilities for the musical and dramatic arts. A

Downe House Seniors' Association

From the early days, former pupils were not forgotten once they had left school. News of their lives after school, including their addresses, was regularly included in the school magazines. Somewhat confusingly, every girl on leaving is called a Senior or Old Senior even if she had not actually been a Senior (prefect) while at school. An Association of Seniors, the DHSA, was formed quite early on, with a voluntary membership. The record keeping was done in an *ad hoc* way, with an honorary committee aided by one or more representatives from each year, known as the registrars. The main event each year was the return to school for Seniors' Weekend.

In 1946 the DHSA, while retaining the basic structure of voluntary committee and registrars, was put on a more formal basis. It celebrated its Golden Jubilee in 1996 and has continued to flourish. It issues in alternate years 'News from Old Seniors' and a comprehensive 'Address List', the cost of these and other benefits being covered by the lifetime subscription paid while at school. Many contributors to this book have paid tribute to the lasting friendships made at school, and the DHSA has played its part in enabling girls to keep in touch.

As the numbers increased, the administration, mostly on card indices maintained by worthy volunteers, became an onerous task and an offer from the school to help by appointing and housing an administrator was gratefully received. Joanne Ray set to work with the committee and the registrars, and in a relatively short time had computerised the database and found many previously 'lost' former pupils. She also dealt with the problems endemic for societies dealing with Old Girls, who so often change their names on marriage/remarriage/divorce, by managing to train DHSA members to notify all changes of name or address to school. This has greatly helped her successor, who has also taken advantage of the school's centenary to improve the records and the archives of the school. By the time this book is published, the vast majority of the DHSA will have had the opportunity to attend decade reunions held at the school during the past four years. The enthusiastic response generated by these innovations has been astonishing. The DHSA, with President Susan Sinclair and Chairman Gillian Hulbert, is still run by a voluntary committee representing all ages, and by the registrars. It still fulfils its original aims, to maintain contacts between old girls, to help with grants towards worthwhile ventures after school, and to help the school whenever possible.

Kate Finlay

Sixth Form centre has also been constructed out of the old maintenance buildings, and there is a new Medical Centre as well as a new school shop.

Olive Willis would certainly recognise her school at the core of Downe House today, in terms both of the buildings and of the underlying character of the place; and she would also surely accept that the changes to her regime made necessary by the forces of modernisation and progress are good and right. She was, after all, a progressive and intuitive woman who, above all, wanted the best for her 'children'. While her legacy lives on, it is the present Headmistress's vision for the present and the future which is shaping Downe House at the beginning of the twenty-first century.

Downe was fantastic in the way everyone was recognised for their achievements in whatever field. End of term Assembly was a terrific way in which those who had earned sports colours, good academic results, dramatic success, or charity work could stand up in front of the school and be congratulated. The one thing I thank the school most for, however, is the good friendships it allowed me to form. As my peers and I come to the end of a year that held a number of twenty-first birthday celebrations, I'm reminded that the large number of close friends I made during my school days will remain so.

Clare Michell (2002)

Generations and links

There are many multi-generation families to be found in the records of Old Seniors at Downe House – too many to list though some of them feature elsewhere in this book and records of all of them can be found in the school Archives. One of these families is pictured (right): Elizabeth Elwes (Crawley, 1931) with her daughter, Henrietta Metters (Elwes, 1970), and her grand-daughter, Emma Metters (2000). Many reminiscences contain information such as 'I had five cousins with me at school, and my maternal great-aunts were both there, as well as my father's aunt' (Sarah Ingram (King, 1973)). Clare Slemeck (1972) and her sister Nicola Slemeck (1974) can trace their involvement with Downe to Olive Willis's very first pupil Nan Napier (Woodall, 1910), who was their grandmother, via their mother Diana Slemeck (Williamson-Napier, 1937). Fiona McNeill (1993) writes, 'Long before I ever actually saw Downe, my ideas of what to expect were shaped, completely inaccurately, by my grandmother's reminiscences of Downe in the austere 1920s, my mother's and aunt's of the impossibly remote 1950s and 1960s, and those of various great-aunts and cousins throughout the school's history.' Her mother, Anna McNeill (Fogg-Elliot, 1957), adds 'Miss Willis was a great inspiration to my mother, who was at the school in the 1920s. My mother, Margaret Fogg-Elliot (Peel, 1929), and one of her sisters went on to Oxford, quite a feat in those days. My sister, Sarah Seamark (Fogg-Elliot, 1964), followed me there, and my daughter too, so Downe is very much part of all our lives.'

Juliet Austin (Prior, 1962) was Miss Willis's great-niece, a pupil during Miss Medley's time,

and a member of staff under Mrs Wilson and Miss Farr: 'I had two official encounters with Downe but my links with it are much deeper and more complicated than the transfer of hats from pupil to teacher. My parents were married in the Chapel at Downe in 1937 and then in 1944, after my mother escaped from the London air raids to stay with my grandmother on Red Shute Hill, I was born in the bursar's car on the way to the maternity hospital in Reading. Granny was Patience Godfrey, the youngest sister of Aunt Olive, as we knew Olive Willis. Her husband Charles Godfrey, Headmaster of the Naval College at Osborne, had helped Olive set up the original school at Downe in Kent. My mother and her two sisters had been pupils in the early Cold Ash days and my grandmother, when widowed, settled in Hermitage and became a lynchpin of the cello section of the orchestra and close friend of many of the staff.

'I returned to teach on a whim when Mrs Wilson offered me head of the English department. These were difficult years. Mrs Wilson had rescued the school after the illness of Mrs Bourdillon and brought it great energy and clarity of vision. By 1972, however, she was struggling and eventually Suzanne Farr took over and the learning curve began all over again. Friends on the staff warned me that I would be seen as the "old guard", as Aunt Olive's niece and a past pupil, but I never felt that was the case. Miss Farr knew the school needed turning round and suddenly it became again the dynamic and exciting environment that I had found it as a

pupil. Miss Farr was utterly different from Aunt Olive except for two things: she had a passion for education and a passion for dogs. I have an exercise book in which Aunt Olive wrote some of her thoughts on education, and I can imagine her being delighted that Downe was being led by someone who shared her determination that girls should be open to all the intellectual, scientific, and social development of their generation. Openness and flexibility of mind and attitude were self evident in all that Aunt Olive did, and Miss Farr too epitomised it in her determination that pupils should have the very best education that she could possibly achieve. Above all, she wanted them to think for themselves. The Downe of today is deeply impressive and I am full of admiration for the results it achieves and the enterprise of its pupils, evident from the school magazines. I hope two things for current pupils. The first is that the true love of reading for its own sake, not just for examinations, is still at the heart of its teaching. The second is that any girl who wishes to take her goat to a local agricultural show, should, as in Aunt Olive's day, be allowed to do so.'

165

1925 and 2006

Epilogue

Emma McKendrick

So what of the future – Downe House's next hundred years? This book bears vivid witness to the qualities that have made the school what it is: a strong commitment to individuality; an emphasis on service; academic excellence; high-level sporting prowess; magnificent musical and dramatic achievements. Downe House has consistently turned out girls who are confident and assured, well-rounded in all areas of life, and blessed with the lifelong friendships they forge here. The present and the future belong primarily to them, and I am proud of the ways in which they often make a real difference – and proud, too, of the ways in which our highly committed staff guide them through their sometimes challenging adolescent years.

It goes without saying that a wide education in academic subjects remains fundamental. But at the same time the joy of learning outside the classroom is vital, particularly perhaps in an age when many of the girls will go on to study or work abroad and therefore need to appreciate and understand other countries and cultures. We continue to offer lecture programmes on a wide variety of topics, both within the school and through external visits, as well as additional stimuli, for example our annual Literary Festival. To complement the academic curriculum, it is now routine for girls to participate in the Young Enterprise scheme, the Model United Nations, the Duke of Edinburgh Award Scheme, and Debating, and to take part in curriculum visits at home and overseas. Recent visits to India, China, Borneo, Canada, South Africa, and many European countries ensure that horizons are kept broad.

The sense of service too, so much part of Olive Willis's vision, is embedded in Downe. We are constantly looking at ways in which we can make a difference to our local community and, in small ways, to the wider world. Girls regularly visit and help at the Castle School, a school for children with special needs, and Priors Court, a school for autistic children, as well as visiting the elderly at the local Old People's Home and helping in local charity shops and the local Sunday school. In the wider world, we are in the process of setting up links with schools in South Africa, Sri Lanka, Romania, Malaysia, Uganda, and South America. Each House is to have a particular link with a school in the developing world, with the aim of raising awareness, increasing understanding and tolerance of other countries and cultures, appreciating the diversity of the world, and seeing where they can make a difference.

When I first came to Downe, I noticed and commented on the 'buzz' of the school – the spirit that makes Downe special. Crucial to this buzz are the relationships between staff, pupils, Governors, old girls, domestic staff – everyone who is part of the school. These relationships are based on mutual respect; the ability, for example, of the girls and staff to let their hair down in one another's company at the Staff Pantomime or a Charity Staff Fashion Show never disturbs the effective working relationships in the classroom or the normal parameters of courtesy to be seen around the school. Within the pupil body too, the girls work together, learn to respect each other's differences, and appreciate each other's strengths and weaknesses. Friendships remain very strong indeed, and girls regularly greet each other after

168

Two school photographs: the earliest, in 1909, and the latest, in 2005

an exeat as if they have been separated for at least six months! In addition, the Seniors and members of the Anti-Bullying Committee, the School Council, the Food Committee, and House Committees all play a significant part in creating their environment, contributing to and taking responsibility for the management of their school. And our excellent Governing Body, led by George Inge, Chairman 1999–2004, and Nigel Rich, Chairman since 2004, watch over us well, supporting the school with their strong interest in all that happens and guiding us with a light but expert

touch which never allows complacency to be a word associated with the management or leadership of Downe.

There are, of course, challenges ahead. Technology is developing at an alarming rate and its impact on our teaching, learning, and living cannot be underestimated. The secret will remain that of ensuring that we take the best from the developments to enhance every aspect of school life. The pressure to maintain up-to-date facilities and high standards is likely to be ever-present, and finances have to be managed accordingly. We have to deal also with the rather too regularly changing curriculum demands imposed by various Government initiatives. And fundamentally, the value and future of independent, single-sex, boarding education remains under scrutiny by the Government, its agencies, the media, and of course current and future parents and pupils. The only certainty for the future is that there will continue to be change and that it is unlikely to slow down! Downe has to be in a position to respond to those changes in

order to ensure that it remains at the forefront of girls' boarding education. We cannot stand still, for this surely means that we will go backwards; we must continue to develop and move forwards. We must continue to strive for excellence in all that we undertake, hold firm to our core Christian values, and ensure that the breadth of education we offer enables the young women who leave aged eighteen-plus to play a full part in society. My hope is that the girls will leave confident that they have the academic and personal skills to stride out and face the challenges of a very fast-changing world. Equally important, however, is my hope that this confidence will be balanced with a humility that makes them caring, sensitive colleagues, professionals, leaders, friends, wives, mothers, and members of the wider community. Far less challenging to write down than to achieve in reality!

Finally, I must speak of our ethos – still rooted in Olive Willis's vision but developed, strengthened, and moved on by so many charismatic and committed men and women since. We were worried, at the recent ISI Inspection, that the Inspectors might not understand this very strong ethos. We needn't have been. Let their words sum up our first century and our hopes and expectations for the next:

'The school's major strength is its ethos. It is a community displaying strong values, appropriate patterns of behaviour, good relationships, and mutual respect between individuals of all ages. The ways in which the school achieves this special quality are complex, but are exemplified by effective leadership, insistence on high standards of behaviour, meaningful assemblies, spiritual awareness, and knowledge of the outside world as well as of the school itself. The happy, relaxed atmosphere of the school encourages pupils to relate constructively to one another, to take responsibility, and participate fully in the school community. The attractive, tranquil site provides an appropriate context for the development of well rounded, mature individuals.'

169

Glossary

Expressions and phrases used in school. Some were in fashion for many years while others had a limited lifespan; some have changed their meaning over time.

Binge Midnight feast

Bogey man A flasher in the woods

Book bags Pale green bags with leather handles (allegedly made by prisoners) marked with one's name and dragged around school stuffed with books, files, etc

Bovvers/Bovver boys Local boys

Braddy laddies/Bradlads Bradfield College boys

Cathedral Steps Steps running down from the Junior House to the old gym

Cells Music practice rooms in the Cloisters

Choral by candlelight At Christmas dinner the lights would be turned off and Choral would process through the darkened Dining Room and Gallery, hidden in their cloaks, singing carols

Cow The self-service milk machine in the Dining Room

Crossed To cross one's knife and fork to reserve a place at the table – generally as far away from the member of staff as possible!

Dead Ants The much-loved game where one person shouts out Dead Ant and everyone lies on their backs on the floor and waves their arms and legs

Field Games, eg House Field

Forty A forty-minute lesson

Foxgroves Much visited sweetshop just along the road past Field

Hedgehog A crisp, rounded meat loaf or minced meatballs

High, the Large table at the top of the Dining Room where the Head or the presiding mistress sat for meals

Janes Loos

Jaw Originally individual talk with Miss Willis or Miss Medley each term; later meeting for all school and staff at the beginning and end of term

Jellybag Brassiere

Lax Lacrosse; although earlier referred to as 'crosse'

Leaving dare Traditional high jinks performed by leavers of each year, eg moving all the tables and chairs out of the Dining Room onto the lawn

Leaving table A table consisting of someone from each year chosen by the leaver for their last few weeks

Lecture dresses A smart dress for chapel, concerts, and public occasions

Long and Short Exeat Never 'half term' always Long Exeat

Ma W/Pammy Mrs Wilson, the Headmistress; other venerable staff had the prefix 'Ma', eg Ma Cas (Madame Castellini)

Middle East etc Names given to parts of the main building; Far East, Top Top South, Middle West, etc

Mufti day A normal school day when the girls are allowed to wear their own clothes rather than uniform, and everyone tries to look individual but ends up looking like everyone else!

Nature trail A marked path created through the woods so that the girls can observe nature

Notices Given out by the Seniors, standing by the pillars in the Dining Room after meals: 'Are there any notices?'

Odey dodey/BO basher Deodorant

Pash An older girl on whom a younger girl had a crush; the younger girl was sometimes expected to make her bed on clean sheets day! The pash would make toast for the younger girl (satellite)

Penny Reading Review, with short performances by girls

Pepper pot The gazebo-type structure below the Cloisters; always features in a new girls' quiz

Purple jersey The coveted garment worn only by the Head Senior – lost in the mid-1990s

Room Bedroom – never a 'dorm' as at other schools

Satellite The younger girl who had a crush on the older girl (the pash)

Saturday shop The bakery and sweet shop in Cold Ash – a good twenty-minute walk but the only shop the girls were allowed to go to on a Saturday

Scrum School train to and from Paddington

Senior School prefect

Seven sisters The 'satellite' lights in the Dining Room; always feature in a new girls' quiz

Sitting first To sit next to the head of table; sitting second was one place away, etc

Squash To have to squeeze onto another table that does not have an empty space

TP Team practice (Games)

Wacky-B A waste paper basket filled with small presents from the rest of the House given to a girl on her birthday; a Downe House tradition to this day

Waitings Waitress duties done by the younger girls; a Remove would be expected to do around three waitings, a Middle Fourth about two, etc

Wandering To be ousted from one's allocated table and have to find a place elsewhere; 'may I wander?' – a nervewracking experience

Wednesday shop Foxgrove Stores in Cold Ash; the only shop the girls were allowed to visit on a Wednesday – their half day

Subscribers

Annabelle P Abbott (née Carter)
Elizabeth Adams (née Acland)
Ginny Adams
Julia Adlard
Ruth Adorian (née Wakefield)
Georgina Agnew
Caroline, Lady Ailesbury
Christian Alexander
Maeve Alexander
Josephine Allen
Alexandra Ames
Miss Hana Merza Amin
Rosemary Andreae (née Gilbert)
 aka Baird
Venetia and Olivia Andrew
Eleanor Argyll (Duchess of,
 née Cadbury)
The Armitage Family
Clare Armstrong (née Iliffe)
Mr and Mrs Stephen Arnott
Brenda Artus Touche
Betsy V Ashton
Karen Ashwood
Ruth Aspinall
Tamara Astor
Rosie Atkins
Joan Atkinson
Coral and Karen Au
Diane Austin (née Norman-Butler)
Heather Austin
Juliet Leathes Austin
Katie Austin
The Hon Julian and Mrs Aylmer

Martha Back
Estela Baden
Patricia Bagshawe (née Crompton-
 Inglefield)
Diana Bailey (née Hughes)
Mrs J Bailey (née Hughes)
Mrs Anne Baker Baker (née Bruen)
Jane Baker (née Dunphie)
Mary Baker
Natasha Baker
Emma Balding (née Hastings-Bass)
Mrs Prudence Balfour
Lara Bampfylde
Susan Band (née Goodenough)
Louie Banham
Flora (Posy) Bankes
Rosanna (Wink) Bankes
Talêri Bankes
Elizabeth Barclay
Charlotte Barker

Lotte Barker-Hahlo
Mrs Diana Barkes
Frances Barnes
Pamela Barnett (née Grant)
Annette Barnsdale-Diffey
Alison Bartholomew (née MacKenzie)
Jacqueline Bartrum
Mrs Joan Bassett (née
 Rainsford-Hannay)
Sheila Bateman (née Gamble)
M E Batstone (née Milford)
Sarah Battey
Susan Batty
Mary Baxter (née Roadnight)
Cassie Bayly
Mrs Simon Bayly (née Christina
 Hindson)
Susan Beale (née Brierley)
Mrs D M Beardsmore (Jennifer
 Gilberton)
Anna Beatson-Hird
Nicola Beckwith
Pollyanna Beeley
Elizabeth Beer (née Dawes)
Pamela M Bellars
Mrs Mary Bellhouse
Esther Bennett (née Pirie)
Tessa Bennett (née Gamble)
Beatrice Bennett
Emily Bennett
Sophie Katharine Bentley
Corrine Bentley-Rawson (née
 McCarthy)
Mrs Marion Bentley-Taylor
Rosemary Biggs (née Harrison)
Sheila Bint
Mrs Mary Bishop
Mrs Rebecca Black
Juliette, Larissa and Elena Blackshaw
Carol Blackwood (née Smith)
Philippa Blowfield (née Henry)
Emma Jane Caroline
 Blyth-Whitelock
Jennie Blyth-Whitelock
Michael Kirk Blyth-Whitelock
Skye Sophie Claudia
 Blyth-Whitelock
Hannah Boase
Emma Bolton
Clodagh Bonham Carter
Mrs L Borradaile
Polly Boswell (née Sowerby)
Livia Boumeester
Lottie Boumeester

Jennifer Bourdillon
Emma Bourne
Julia Bourne (née Cleave)
Alita Bovill
Mrs Olivia Bovill
Louise Bowers
Sarah Bradbury (née Hillier)
Carol Brandl (née Finch)
Elizabeth Breton (née Dean)
Margie Brett (née Robertson)
Miss Olivia Brewer
Libby and Catriona Brewin
Pearl Brewis (née
 Beaumont-Thomas)
Celia Briant
Pamela Bridge
Patricia Brims (née Henderson)
Anna Brooksbank
Mandy Broughton (née Cotton)
Norman Brown
Pamela Brown (née Buchanan)
Patricia Brown
Victoria Brown
Louise Bryan
Ann Budd (née Lawson)
Dr Anne Sheppard
Rosie Bunting
Alison Burgess
Rose Burgess
Laura Burke
Penny Burles (née Reeves)
Diana Burlton (née Prickett)
Lady Burton (née King)
Mr and Mrs Butcher
Sian Butcher
Elizabeth Butler
Laura Buxton
Margaret Buxton
Valerie Byrom-Taylor

Anthony Benedict Cain
Susan Cameron
Mr and Mrs A Cameron
Charlotte Campbell
Katie Campbell
Sophie Campbell
Camilla Capaldi
Bettina Capel (née Rowlands)
(Catherine) Margaret Cardell-Oliver
Major General and Mrs Carlier
Alison Carter (née Budd)
Sophie Casben (née Waggett)
Marina Castronovo (née
 Mohamed-Ariff)

Susanna Catlin (née Dring)
Caroline Cave
Rosemarie Cawson (née Beer)
Edwina Cazenove
Miranda Challen
Anna Chambers (née Lyster)
Caryl Chaplin
Jane Chaplin (née Melville)
Mme F Chartrain
Abigail Chase
Mrs Ruth Chavasse
Carolyn Chaventre (née Hamilton)
Phillida Cheminals (née Milford)
Susan and Diana Chen
Amanda Cherry
Ann Chilton
Miss Monica China
Mrs Gillian Church (née Sankey)
Mrs A Cibula (née Evelyn Elbugen)
Mrs Ann Hazel Cipps
Mr and Mrs Richard Clare
Barbara Clark
Felicity Clark
Brian Clarke
Mrs Elizabeth Clarke (née Wordie)
Theodora Clarke
India Clegg
Mrs Elisabeth Clifford
Olivia Clifton-Bligh
Susan Cobham (née Townsend)
Hebe Cockcroft
Mrs Angela Coghill
Mrs B Cohen
Helena Coles
Mrs N R Colquhoun
Rachel Aline Colville
Bridget Commel (née Fletcher)
Mr David Comyn
Jess Conner
Louisa Constantine
Sheila Constantinidi (née
 Whittington)
Camilla Conybeare-Cross (née Robb)
Kate Cooke (née Tilbury)
Sophie A A Cooke
Carol Cooper
Clio Cooper
Perina Courtauld
Mrs M L Cowper (née Luce)
Mrs Diana Cox (née Ffennell)
Mrs Natalie Cox (née Hatton)
Alicia Crabbe (née Meeke)
Mavis Muir Cragg
Jill Craig (née Davies)

172

Isabel Cronk; Alexandra Cronk
Alix Culberston
Ann Cumming (née Crawford)
Mrs Eva Cummins
Sara Cunningham
Susan Cunningham
Emma Curley

Annabel Dangerfield
Mrs Anne Davenport
Amanda David
Sheila David
Jennifer Davies
Rose Davis (Mrs E B Daubeny)
Fenella Dawnay
Jill de Castella (née Macrae)
Susan de Costobadie
The de Giorgio Family
Mr and Mrs Jeremy de Souza
Victoria de Trense
Lucy Mary Denholm (née Knox)
Dione Dennis (née Sellar)
Imogen Dessain (née Crabtree)
Francesca Devas
Sarah Dewe-Mathews
Mrs D V Dick
Elizabeth Dickson
Bridget Diggens
Henrietta Dillon (née Elwell)
Antonia Dodd-Noble
Cara Doherty
Lucy and Amy Donner
Caroline Douglas-Cooper
Catherine Dowler
Gulielma Dowrick
Frances Dowson (née Green)
Camilla Drinkall
Katrina Druitt
Eleanor Dudley-Williams
Count and Countess Duerckheim
Eugenie Duerckheim
Georgina Duerckheim
Sophie Duerckheim
Clare Duffield (née Davies); Sarah
    Nicholas (née Burton)
Elizabeth Durazzano (née Caldicott)

Justine Earl
Tabitha Eccles
Alethea Eddy
Mary Eld
Mrs J E Ellen
Laurence Ellis
Charlotte Enoch
Margaret Evans (née Hart)
Miss Rosemary Evans

Juliana Fadl
Victoria Fairley (née Sanderson)
Eleanor Fane
Lizzie Fane
Nell Fane
Margery Farr (née Dawson)
Heather Farrer-Brown (née Gale)
Nicola Fazakerley

Mrs Gillian Feary
Emma Fellowes
Susan Fellowes (née Brodhurst-Hill)
Jennifer Fellows (née Rowley)
Libby Fellows
Sophie Ferguson
Emma Fergusson
Mrs Judith Fergusson
Susan Fesko (née Cleaver)
Miss Charlotte Fetiveau
Susan Fiddick (née Smyth)
Mrs Eileen Field (née Gower)
Kate Finlay
Margaret and Nicholas Finney
Honor Fishburn
Mrs Nicola Fitzgerald
Elspeth Fleming
Delle Fletcher
Mrs Elizabeth Anne Flexner
Julia Flint
Anna Flood
Miss E H Foden-Pattinson
Sue Foote
Cazalla Fordham
Lucca Fordham
Diana Foster (née Baillie)
Isobel Fowler
Lorraine Fowler
Rachel Fowler (née Savory)
Constance Fox-Andrews
Jennifer A Francis
Miranda Franks
Sarah Fraser
Georgina Friend

John Gabbitas
Alex Galea
Rohays Galitzine
Jane Gamble
Phyllida Gardner (née Barrow)
Verella Gibb
Diana Gifford Mead (née Collins)
Kitty Gilbert
Caroline Gladstone
Edwina Glennie
Fiona Glennie (née Spencer-Nairn)
Phillida Goad (née Wilson)
Miss Elizabeth Gold
Oriole Goldsmith
Senores de Gonzalez-Barba
Daisy Goodbody
Antonia Goor
Jo Gordon
Iona Gordon Lennox
Nicola Gordon-Finlayson
Mrs Sara Patricia Gorton
Jennifer Gosse
Miss Genevieve Gotla
Mrs J M L Gould (née Acland)
Henrietta Gourlay
Marie-Winter Goury du Roslan
Mrs Sophie Gower (née Hiscocks)
Nicola Gradwell
Clare Graham (née Taylor)
Amber Graham-Watson

Fiona Grant
Stacia F W Grant-Nicholas
Michele Gravenor
Mrs Alexandra Gray (née Maude)
Annabel Gray (née Ludovici)
Elizabeth Gray
Miss Lily L P L Gray
Mr and Mrs Jeffrey Green
Stephanie Green
Susan Greenaway
Dr Alice Greenwood (née
    Bradley-Moore)
Victoria Greenwood
Dinah Gregory
Mia Gregory
Annabel Griffith
Julia Griffith-Jones
Laura Griffith-Jones
Anne Griffiths (née
    Fetherston-Dilke)
Susannah Griffiths
Alicia Grimaldi
Carina Grimaldi
Sophia Grimaldi
Gill Grimes
Kate Guest
Henrietta Gundill (née Stanley)
Juliet Gush
Alison Gwatkin
Janifred Gwynne-Howell (née Waller)

Mr and Mrs Peter Haig
Mrs Jill Haines
Susan Halford (née Williams)
Eleanor Hall
Katherine Hames
Tara Hamilton Stubber
Jill Hamilton-Grierson
Lilly Hanbury
Melissa Hanbury
Alice Hanson
Victoria Hanson
Rachel Louisa Harbron
Heather Harcarik (née Clarke)
Margaret Hardey (née Taylor)
Laetitia Hardie
Catherine Hare (née Verney)
Charlotte Harris
Mrs Jean Harris
Mrs Audrey Harrison
Henrietta Hartley (née Clark)
Julia Haslam
Rev'd Timothy Hastie-Smith
Patricia Paget Hawkes
Mary Haynes (née Lambert)
Lady Anne Hayter
Diana Head
Mrs Linda J Heighway
Iona Hemphill (née Campbell)
Primrose Henderson (née Forrest)
Nelly Galabova Henderson
Belinda Henry
Sheila Hensman
Joanna Heriot Maitland
Janet Hesketh

Julia Hett
Nikki Hickman-Robertson
Mrs Jean Hicks
Harriet Higgins
Jessica Clare Higham (née Acheson)
Lizzie Higham
Chloe Hill
Emma Hill (née McGowan)
Georgina Hill
Nicolas and Mary Hillier
Felicity Hindson
Ms S P Hines
Alison E P Ho
Miss Elizabeth Hoare
Nancy Hoare
Ginny Hobhouse (née Bergen)
Harriet Holder
Jane Holdway
Arabella Hollamby
Lucy Holliday
Jennifer Hollings (née Hutt)
Lucinda Hood
Judith Horner (née Nesbitt)
Caroline Horsbrugh (née Everett)
Sasha Hoskins (née Henderson)
Lady Houssemayne du Boulay
    (Elizabeth Home)
Joan Howard-Jones (née Gilligan)
Anthea Huband
Sally Huband
Anne Huddleston
Carola Hudson
Gillian Hulbert (née Savory)
Nicola Hulbert
Nicola Holt
Mrs Ann M A Humphries
Dr Diana Hunt
Mrs Aminta Hunt
Jenny Hunter
Susan Hutchinson (née Barnes)
Clarissa Hutchinson
Dr Tatiana Hyde

Louisa Ingham
Kate Inglefield
Diana Inskip
Alice Jack
Emily Jack
Mary (née Beckett) and Carolyn Jack
Fiona Jackson
Kizzy Jackson
Liz Jackson
Mrs Emily Jacob
Honor Jacomb-Hood (née Jones)
Geraldine James (née Thomas)
David Jenkins
Pippa Jenkinson (née Rycroft)
Joan Jerrett (née Wernham)
Jan Johnson (née Gay)
Mrs Judy Johnson
Shirley Johnson
Tranquility Johnson
Sara Johnston (née Riddell-Webster)
Hannah Elizabeth Jones
Laura Jones

Patricia Strong Jones
Antonia (Toni) Judd

Mrs Elizabeth Kay (née Owen)
Sue Keate
Fiona Kelly (née Warren)
Georgina Kelly
Janet Kendall (née Hudson)
Annabel Kennedy (née Seccombe)
Ghislaine Kennerley
Caroline Kenny
Jane Kerby (née Middleton)
Anne Keynes (née Adrian)
Caroline Kilner
    (Crompton-Inglefield)
Rosemary Kimmins
Antonia Kingsland
Jennifer Kingsland
Sophie Kinloch
Alethea Knatchbull-Hugessen
Elizabeth Knight (née Clouting)
Elizabeth Knowles (née Townend)
Mrs A Knudsen (née Salter)
Nicola Koo
Jenny Kyle (née Templer)

Annette Lanaghan
Rachel, Rebecca and
    Tamara Lancaster
Morar Lang
Sarah Lang
Vanessa Langdale (née
    Lyndon-Skeggs)
Charlotte Lankston
Lindy Lanning
Frances Lavington-Evans
Mrs M Lawler
Le Quesne Family
Mrs Fiona Leathart
Ann Lee (née Machin)
Barbara Lee (née Roadnight)
Mrs Clare Lee (née Harvey)
Emily Lee (née Baxter)
Mrs Meryan Lee
Mrs C J Leeder
Georgina Leeming (née Large)
Annabelle Lees
Jane Lefever (née Henry)
Elizabeth Leslie (née Bowden-Smith)
Joanna Lewin-Harris
Jill Lewis (née Bradfield)
Victoria and Abigail Lewis
Alison Linklater-Bentley
Col Jonathan Lloyd
Jenny Lloyd-Jacob
Patricia Lockwood
Jane Lovell (née Dorrell)
Miss Jen Mae Low
Eleanor Lucas
Georgina Ludlow
Samantha and Hillary Lui
Lucy Lukic
Cecilia Lunn
Annabelle Lupton
James Lupton

Isma Lutyens
Jenny Lyall Grant (née Moore)
Katherine E Lyell
Penelope Lykiardopulo
Holly Lyne
Nicolette Lyne (née Finzi)
Robert Lynes

Hattie MacAndrews
Teresa MacColl
Mrs Ian MacFarlane
Mrs Paula Machin
Judy Mack
Maureen MacKenzie (née
    Bradish Ellames)
Celia Mackintosh of Mackintosh
    (née Bruce)
Sophy Maclean
A W Macmillan Douglas
Eleanor MacNair
Susan MacPherson (née Perry)
Kinvara Mactaggart
Alexandra Madeley
Victoria Madeley
Alice Magnay (née Lynne)
Hannelore Maier
Mrs Joanna Mains
C Mainwaring-Burton
Mary and David Male
Sharm Malherbe
Georgina Mallows; Rosanna
    Mallows; Caroline Mallows
Anna Maltzoff (née
    Hely Hutchinson)
Martha Mankowitz
Poppy Mankowitz
Mrs Alex Manners
Anna Markwell
Madeline Marriage
Susan Marsden-Smedley (née King)
Louisa Marsh
Judith Marshall formerly Tomlin
    (née Miller)
Mrs Heidi Marvin (née Cooper)
Eleanor Matheson
Annabel Matterson
Anne Moffatt (née Tomlinson)
Mrs K R Maxwell-Hyslop (née Clay)
Rachel Maxwell-Hyslop
Olivia Maynard (née Reed)
Nicky McArthur
Meriel Lane (née McCarthy)
Sarah James (née McCarthy)
Hester McClintock (née Wilder)
Pippa McCosh
Vivian McCoubrey
Mrs K McCulloch
Rosemary McDougal
Mary Ellen McEuen (née Higginson)
Kiloran McGrigor
Mrs Emma McKendrick
Anna McNeill (née Fogg-Elliot)
Fiona McNeill
Julia (Judy) McSwiney
Amanda Mead

Lucy Melford (née Billington)
Marion Mellett
Mrs Elizabeth Melly
Katharine Melville
Charlotte Menon (née Ryder)
Elizabeth Menzies-Wilson (née
    Juckes)
Emma Elizabeth Metters
Henrietta Metters (née Elwes)
Claire Meyer
Mrs Natasha Meynell (née King)
Clare Michell
Phylida Middlemiss (née Cheyne)
Mary Midgley (née Scrutton)
Sara Isabella Miles
Catherine Miller (née
    Marsden-Smedley)
Eve Miller (née Latham)
Kate Milne
Alison Mitchell
Mrs Noah Mitchell
Philippa Mitchell (née Lees)
Mr and Mrs Roger Mitchell
Anne Mitford-Slade
Mary Molesworth-St Aubyn
Mrs Elizabeth Monk and
    Anstace Monk
Georgina Monkland
Carolyn Moore (née Mitford-Slade)
Elly and Simon Moore
Patricia Moore
Joanna More (née Cherry)
Mrs J E Morgan
Lindsey Morgan
Bobbie Morris
Patricia Morris
Sandra Morris
Mrs Tracey Morton (née Moyse)
Wayne Mosher
Juliet Moss (née Rowe)
Olivia Mossop
Olivia Muir
Charlotte Mundy
Pamela Mure
Isabel Murray (née Milne Home)
Mrs Jennifer Murray

Mitsuko Nakajima
Diana Napier
Francesca Nardone
Mrs A Nash
Fiona and Nicola Neilson
Mrs Michelle Newton
Amelia G Nichols
Eleanor Nicholson
Isobel Nicholson
Mary E M Nicholson
Rosamond Nicholson
Zoe and Henrietta Nicholson
Lucy Nicole
Tamsyn Noble (née Pollard)
Rebecca Norris
Ruth Norton
Mrs Pippa Nott
Wendy Nurser

Rosanna Oldham
Sally Oliver (née Exner)
Jeffie Openshaw
Olivia Openshaw
Sarah Orr (née Chappell)
Anna Osmaston (neé Weir)

Jacqueline Packard
Alexander Palfrey and Georgia Palfrey
Catherine Palmer (née Jackson)
Anna Palys
Rachel Parker (née Urwin)
Dr Fiona Parsons
Poosie Parsons
Lucasta Partridge-Hicks
Mrs Nick Paterson (Sara Hobbs)
Rosanna Patrick
Harriet Pattinson
Joan Payne (née Hobhouse)
Margaret Payne
Katherine Peake
Mrs Patricia R Pearce
Lucy Pearson
Lucinda Peat
Rosamond Peirson
R C Pelham Burn
Mrs J Pelly (née Horton-Fawkes)
Charlotte Pemberton
Diana Peper
Gabbie Perkins
Margaret M Perkins (née Marsden)
Sarita Perkins (née Le Grice)
Elizabeth Perring Evans (née Barnes)
Victoria Rose Persson (née Colman)
Mrs Kate Petter
Jane Pettit
Melanie Phillips (née Denham-Davis)
Patricia Phillips (née Hurford)
Shirley Phipps (née Medley)
Saranne Piccaver (née Prior)
David Piper
Mr R G Piper
Diana Pitt (née Lovel Mack)
Sarah Pointon (née Meeke)
Stella Poole
A Popplewell
Jane Portal (née Williams)
Christine Porter
Miss J Powell
Rosemary E Powell (née James)
Rachel and Emma Powell
Sally Pownall (née Deverell)
Daphne Preston
Valerie Preston-Dunlop
Isabel Priestley
Laura Priestley
Rosanna Priestley
Katherine Simpson de Robeck Proby
Pandora Pugsley
Aldena Pyne

Tessa Quartermaine
Ann Quin

Jane Ramage

174

Amanda Ramsay
Amy Ramsay
Amy Rand
Georgina Rawkins
Griselda Rawlinson
Joanne Ray
Catherine Rayner
Erica Read
Sophie Read
Elizabeth Rees (née Calder)
Emily Rees Jones
Juliet Rees Jones
Nikki Reeves
Susan Reid (née Clement)
Lenore Reynell
Lady Rhys Williams
Cynthia Rich (née Davies)
Clare Richards
Gillian Richards
Sarah and Charlotte Richards
Geri Rider (née Woodrow)
Margaret Riley (née Cameron)
Clare Risoe
Paul Risoe
Annabel Ritchie
Joanna Ritchie (née Fletcher)
Keith Robbins
D J Roberts
Patricia R Roberts
Mrs R Roberts
R, S, and D Robins
Celia and Lucy Robinson
Jan Robinson
Mrs Bianca Robson
Laura Robson
Diane Rogers
Sheila Rolland
Amy Ropner
Cordelia Rosa
Jessie Rose
Annabel Ross
Elizabeth Rowley
Poppy Royal
Abigail Rudd
Emma Runge
Alicia Russell
Elizabeth Russell (née Mynors)
Emily, Kitty and Alice Russell
Talitha Russell

Jessica Sainsbury
Nathalie Salm
Graham Salter
Mrs Sylvia Sandeman
Laura Sanderson
Mrs Susan Sanderson
Lady Catherine Sandford (née Hunt)
Stephanie Sargent
Carol Sarsfield-Hall
R C Sarsfield-Hall
Kate Savage
Sheila Saxby-Soffe
Susan Schanche (née Gaddum)
Mr and Mrs L F Schultz
Erica Schumacher

Francisca Sconce
Mrs M A Scott
Michael R Scott
Victoria Scott
Katie-Claire Scrivener
Sara Scrivener
Chloe Searle
Robin Sedgwick
Caroline Sellon (née Marriott)
Mrs Jane Selwyn Bailey (née Selwyn)
Mrs Mark Sewell
Sheila Shannon
Miss Rosie Shaw
Gillian Sheldon
Josephine Shenkman
Nina Shenkman
Jackie Shepherd-Cross
Sally Shewell
Melanie Shingles (née Stuttaford)
Olympia Shivdasani
Marcelle Siddall
Samantha Simmonds (née Thomson)
Kristin and Karl Simpson
Julia Simpson-Orlebar
Helen Sinclair
Susan Sinclair
Georgina Smee
Mrs Moyra Smiley (née Scott)
Christine Smith
Fiona Smith (née Sinclair)
Tessa Smith (née Kempton)
Tessa Smith
Deirdre Smithwick
Elizabeth Sola
Christina Sola
Melissa Somerville
Elizabeth Sowerby
Lucy Speelman
Ohmar Spence
Victoria Spence
Bridget Spencer (née Goulding)
Margaret E Spicer
Janet Spicer
Tony Stacey
Mr and Mrs P A Stack
Martin and Georgina Stanley
Penelope Starey
Mrs Anthea Steel (née Wilson)
Sophie Steel
Lucy Steen
Charlotte Stephen
Kate Stephen
Nicola Sterry
Rebecca Stevenson
Serena Stevenson (née Pelly)
Sophia Stirling
Isabella F Stopford
Carola Stormonth Darling (née Erskine-Hill)
Philippa Strang
Doreen Strange
Mrs Josephine M C Street
Mr and Mrs Stretton
Jane Strudwick (née Godson)

Nicola Sutherland
Margie Sutton Nelthorpe
Mrs Helen Swinnerton (née Rowley)

Michelle H W Tam
Charlotte Tavener
Rachel Tavener
Carolyn Taylor (née Medley)
Cynthia Taylor (née Acland)
Helen Taylor
Linda Taylor
Mary Taylor (née Beck)
Nancy Taylor
Sarah Taylor (née East)
Camilla ter Haar
Mrs Angela Thomas
Emily V Thomas
Penny Thomas (née Hogg)
Victoria Thomas (née Trotter)
Michael Thompson
Sue Thompson (née Hammerton)
Alice Thomson
Elizabeth Thomson
Patience Thomson
Ann Tidy
Joan Tilley (née Fulton)
Laura Tindley
Lucinda Tindley (née Franks)
Sophie Tindley
Susan Titley
Dr Annabel Todd
Emma Tomlinson
Lucinda Torrance
Rosie Townsend
Susan Treadwell (née Sellors)
Carolyn Trollope (née Gardner)
Mary Alice Trustram Eve
Miss C Tye

Patsorn Udomritthiruj

Mr and Mrs M Van der Gucht
Emily and Francesca Van Oss
Karen Van Poznak (Springthorpe)
Bobyl Vann
Dasha Varvarina
Sophia Vaughan
Jo Vellascott
Caroline Voaden

Susanna Waddington
Jo Waddington
Zoe Wakefield
Eliza Wakefield
Patricia Wakeford
Melissa Wakeley
Annie Walker (née Fellowes)
Georgina Walker
Hilary Walker
Jenny Walker
Delicia Wallace (née Curtis)
Lucy Wallace
Jennifer D C Wallinger
Janet Walton Masters (née MacKenzie-Edwards)

Katharine Ward (née Morrison)
Emma Waterhouse
Lucy Webb
Sarah Webster
The Hon Mrs Wedgwood (née MacLehose)
Mrs Elaine Wells
Olivia (Bridgie) Wells
Vicky Wells
Mary West
Mrs V K Westacott
Nicola Westropp
Mrs Bridget Wheeler (née Campbell)
Mrs Peter Whitamore
Hannah Leonora May Whitehead
Diane Whitehead
Mr and Mrs Mark Whitehead
Jennifer Whitehouse-Vaux
Jonquil Una Whitelock
Florence Whittaker
Mrs Olivia Whitworth (née Colman)
Araminta Wieloch
Cassandra Wiener (née Donner)
Bridget Wijnberg
Mrs Jane Wijsman (née Swettenham)
Ann Wilkinson (née Waterston)
Barbara Williams (née Greenlees)
Caroline Williams
Charlotte Williams
Elizabeth, Lady Williams (née Bond)
Harriet M M Williams
Victoria Williams
Rachel Willis Fleming (née Hollins)
Albinia Willis (née Oldfield)
Jane E S Willis
Victoria Willis
Mrs Juliet Wills
Carolyn Wilson (née Reid)
Prue Wilson (née Attwood)
Jill Wolfe (née Davis)
Audrey Wong
Amelia Wood
Cynthia Wood (née Boot)
Jo Wood
Mrs Katie Wood
Susan Wood (née Chenevix-Trench)
Rosey Woodbridge (née Handley)
Sue Woodroffe (née Farrer)
Sue Woodward
Priscilla Woolworth
Avril Wotherspoon (née Edwards)
Clare Wright
Deborah Wright (née Allen)
Fiona Wright (née Cowan)
Hannah Wright
Alexandra Wyatt
Charlotte Wyatt
Olivia Wyld
A M Wyllie
Libby Wyman

Lisa Yagasaki
Judy Yendole (née Hickson)
M E Young
Christina Yen Ting Yuen

Index of Names and Topics

Names

Bold text denotes authorial contributions. Italics denote illustrations.

Adam, Rosanne (née Watson) 71, 72
Adams, Elizabeth (née Acland) 84
Agobert, Mlle 34, 121
Ailesbury, Caroline (née Wethered) 58
Aitken, Laura 105
Alderton, Pat 84
Allin, Rev Philip 33
Altham, Rowena (née Portal) 42, 46
Andreae, Rosemary (née Gilbert) **75**
Argyll, Eleanor (née Cadbury) **158**
Artus, Brenda (née Touche) 108
Aspinall, Ruth 54
Austin, Sister 47
Austin, Juliet (née Prior) 98, **164–65**
Austin, Anthony 98

Baber, Jocelyn (née Ashley Dodd) 6, 15, 17, 19, **20**
Bacon, Paula 69
Baker, Sophie **73**
Balding, Clare 34, *112*
Bannister, Julia (née Talbot-Rice) **79**
Barbirolli, Evelyn (Lady) (née Rothwell) 84, 105–6
Barnett, Lady (née Pamela Grant) 98
Barnsley, Miss ('the Barn') 62, 69, 122, 156
Bartrum, Jacqueline 98
Bate, Miss 62
Bateman, Sheila (née Gamble) 51
Batstone, M E (née Milford) **63**, 84
Batstone, Angela 114, 131
Bayliss, Jack 114, **128–31**, *128*, 131, 133, *143*
Beale, Susan (née Brierley) 85
Berwick, Lynne 103, 133, 136
Bewick, Miss 62
Birnie, Alex **97**
Blakiston, Caroline 69
Blowfield, Philippa (née Henry) 158
Bonham-Carter, Sibella 18
Bottomley, Virginia 114
Bourdillon, Jennifer *73*, 74, 78, 123, *159*, 165
Bowen, Elizabeth 6, **20**
Bradley-Moore, Dr 47, 66
Brewis, Pearl (née Beaumont-Thomas) 44, 109
Britz, Sister 47
Brown, Sue 125
Budd, Ann (née Lawson) **74**

Burgess, Alison (née Cummings) **67**
Butcher, Josephine *89*, 100
Butt, Sarah (née Richardson) 111–12
Buxton, Margaret (née Bridges) 62
Byrom-Taylor, Valerie **87–9**, *89*, 90, 100

Cain, Anthony 90
Cameron, Susan 17, *131*, **148–51**, *154*, **156–59**, 156, 159
Campbell, Bridget **97**
Carter, Alison (née Budd) **64**
Carver, Alice 12, 13, *14*, 108
Castellini, Barbara 114
Charteris, Miss 43
Cheeseman, Margaret 160
Clouting, Sister 47
Coffee, John 161
Colebrook, Susan 118
Collins, Miss 13
Colombani, Natalia 38
Conran, Sir Terence 107
Coombs, Rev John 33
Crawford, Betty (née Studholme) 31
Croft, Winona ('Caw', 'Crift') **20**, 21, 31, 62, 75

Darley, Mary 36
Davies, Joan (née Cooke) *74*
Dawson, Frances (née Green) 23
Dawson, Mrs 80
de Albuquerque, Sophie **160**
Deacon, Tony 101
Denham-Davies, Melanie **97**
Dennis, Diana (née Sellar) 38
Dennis, Katherine 38
Dickson, Elizabeth 40, **64**
Doherty, Elizabeth 97, *99*
Dowrick, Gulielma (née Lister) 34
du Pre, Hilary 73
du Pre, Jacqueline 73, 84

Edey, Celia (née Green) 24, 42
Ellen, Janet (née Pearson) 16
Elsie (school gardener) 30, 160
Elwes, Elizabeth (née Crawley) *164*
Emson, Camilla, *Abstract 144*
Evans, Rosemary 89, 140
Eve, Belinda (née Stobart) 39

Fairbank Miss ('Fizzy') 84
Farr, Suzanne 17, 19, 25, 39, 80, 89, **93–119**, *94*, *96*, 99, 100, 109–10, 113, *119*, 123–24, 128, 131, 132, 137, 156, *159*, 161, 165
Farrar, Sheila 48

Fazakerley, Nicky **97**
Feary, Gillian (née Brundell) **67**
Ffennell, Diana **97**
Field, Eileen (née Gower) 84
Fiennes, Sir Ranulf 114
Finlay, Kate **163**
Finzi, Hilary 100
Finzi, Nico 103
Fischer-Williams, Mariella (née Williams) 33
FitzGerald, Nicola (née Norman-Butler) 108
Fleming, Amaryllis 84
Fletcher, Delle (née Chenevix-Trench) 16, **47**
Fogg-Elliot, Margaret (née Peel) 164
Foote, Sue 125, 146
Francis, Jeremy 105
Frankland, Stephanie 90
Freeman-Attwood, Marigold (née Philips) **50**

Gadd, Alfred 17
Gibbs, Alison 160–61
Gifford Mead, Diana (née Collins) 46
Gill, Margaret 118
Godfrey, Patience (née Willis) 165
Godfrey, Charles 165
Goode, Dorothy 118, *119*
Gosse, Jennifer 17, 55, 75, 78, 117, 156–57, *156*
Gould, Joan (née Acland) 38
Grant, Peter 105
Gray, Annabel (née Ludovici) **98**, 99, **101**
Gray, Elizabeth **113**
Green, Deirdre (née Cain) **67**
Greenwood, Alice (née Bradley-Moore) **66**
Griffiths, Alexandra (née Squires) 102
Grimes, Gill (née Townend) 23
Guest, Kate **144**
Guinness, Katherine 158
Gunn, Marjorie 17, *20*, 34, 48, 63, 82–85, *83*, 86, 90
Gunn, Mary Rose 55
Gunn, Sazzie 84, 90
Gwatkin, Alison 118, *119*, **132–35**, 135, *159*, 160

Hacking, Joanna **157**
Harkness, Juliet (née Wilson) **76**
Harvey, Rev Dr Anthony 159
Hattie (seamstress) 24
Hatton, Sandra 143
Hatton, Virginia 69
Haughton, Jane 143
Havergal, Miss *20*
Heather, Lilian 13, *14*, 15, *20*, 34, 37, 38, 49, 121, 122
Henderson, Primrose (née Forrest) 52
Henriques, Miss 64
Hesketh, Janet (née Laurie) 72
Hess, Dame Myra 34, 48, 54, 66, 83–84, 88
Hicks, Debbie 125
Hickson, Miss 62

Hill, Elizabeth (née Gardner) 90
Hitchcock, Luella *144*
Hoare, Nancy 43
Hodgkin, Professor Dorothy 74, *75*, 123
Holdway, Jane 160
Hollings, Jennifer (née Hutt) 22, 53, **61**
Holmes, Jim 161
Hooper, Denny 146
Horner, Judith (née Nesbitt) **70**
Horsbrugh, Caroline 65
Horsburgh, Miss 102
Houghton, Eileen 114
Houssemayne du Boulay, Elizabeth (née Home) 16
Howard, Jenny 158
Hubback, Judith (née Williams) 34, **43**, 121
Hulbert, Gillian (née Savory) 25, 39, 40, 163
Hulbert, Nicola (née Stobart) **71**
Hunter, Sister 47

Ilford, Betty (née Cotton) *160*
Ingram, Sarah (née King) 164

Jack, Carolyn 72
Jackson, Elizabeth (née Hall) 52
James, Geraldine (née Thomas) 42, 69, **72**, 109
Jerrett, Joan (née Wernham) 64
Johnson, Shirley 160
Jones, Patricia (née Strong) **71**
Jukes, Elizabeth 108–9

Kellow, Mr 103
Kennet, Elizabeth (née Adams) 49
Kielly, Pam 69
Kimmins, Rosemary **87**, 116
Kingsland, Jennifer 117, 125, **145–47**
Kite, Sister 47, 60, 67, 72
Knowler, Elizabeth (née Townend) 23
Krasinska, Anna (née Molesworth-St Aubyn) 7

Lancaster, Patricia 102
Lane, Miss 13
Lee, Gillian (née Hill) **79**
Lee, Melissa **159**
Leeming, Nina (née Large) **162**
Leggo, Rosie (née Bunting) **78**
Leicester, Colonel J Holditch ('Nunky') *36*
Lepper, Charles 117
Lewin, Miss 62
Lewis, Jill (née Bradfield) 16, **44**
Lill, John 88
Linklater, Alison 6
Lister, Margaret (née Pryor) 24, 34
Lockwood, Pat 161
Lord, Hannah *144*
Lucas, Audrey 108
Lunn, Cecilia 87, 89
Lympany, Moura 88

Machin, Paula (née Pritchard) 110
Maclean, Mamie 109

Maclure, Patrick *105*
Macnair, Eleanor 32
Madame (Aganita Houlberg) *20*, 45, 55, 60, *63*, *163*
Maier, Hannelore 52
Main, Susan (née Chaplin) **73**
Markwell, Anna **97**, 102
Marsden-Smedley, Susan (née King) **51**
Maxwell Knight, Susi 96
Maxwell-Hyslop, Rachel (née Clay) **42**
McClintock, Hester (née Wilder) **37**
McCosh sisters, the *111*
McCulloch, Katharine (née Inglis) **39**, 84
McGrigor, Emma (née Fellowes) **100**
McKendrick, Emma 134, *159*, **160–61**
McMaster, Ian 63
McNeill, Anna (née Fogg-Elliot) 164
McNeill, Fiona 164
Medley, Nancy ('the Med') *19*,39, 42, 51, 58, 60, **62**, 63, 64, 67, 70, 72, 73, 75, 76, 77, 109, 156
Mellett, Marion *160*
Metters, Emma *164*
Metters Henrietta (née Elwes) *164*
Meyer, Claire 86
Michell, Claire **163**
Middlemiss, Phyllida (née Cheyne) 105
Midgley, Mary (née Scrutton) 15, 30, 42, 68, 121
Milford, Marion 85
Milford, Robin 83
Miller, Eve (née Latham) 122
Mitchell, Alison 60
Mitchell, Miss 96
Molesworth-St Aubyn, Mary (née Meiklejohn) **7**
Montgomery, Flora 69
Moore, Alice 14
Moore, Mrs 14
Moore, Mary 114, *119*, 133, **136–40**, 140, 149, 159
Moore, Ralph 14, 66
Morgan, Dr 47
Morgan, Mrs 113
Morgan, Rosemary 146
Morgan-Brown, Winifred **12**, 14, 18, *20*
Morris, Joanna (née Woodhouse) **80**
Morrissey, Katharine **159**
Moses, Ruth 49
Mosher, Wayne 161
Murphy, Mary (née Pierce) 41, **78**
Murray, Dame Rosemary 74, *75*, *107*, 113

Naismith, Mary *143*
Napier, Priscilla (née Hayter) 13, 18, 34, 45
Napier, Nan (née Woodall) **14**, 16, 164
Nelthorpe, Clare 159
Nickel, Maria 14, *15*, 16, 18, 20, 28, 31, 45, 48, 98, 103, 113
Nowell-Smith, Elizabeth 122–23
Nowell-Smith, Isabel 104

Oldham, Rosanna 125
Oldham, Mrs 131
Oliver Miss *20*
Owen, Elizabeth 114

Packer, Tom 118
Palmer, Cherry 54
Palmer, Elizabeth *58*, 58–60
Parsons, Fiona 33
Payne, Margaret 52
Payne, John 110
Peirson, Rosamund (née Hoare) 83
Peper, Diana (née Selby) 19
Perkins, Caroline (née McCutcheon) 41, **76**
Persson, Rose (née Colman) 81
Piper, Reg 36
Plowden, Lady 124
Pocock, Mr 67, 79
Pocock, Maud 103
Poore, Mamie 49, 121
Powell, Rosemary (née James) **38**, 84
Preston Dunlop, Valerie (née Preston) 108
Pryor, Julia 34
Pyke, Constance 70, 77

Rae, Fiona 142
Ray, Joanne 163
Rayne, Lydia 111
Read, Dorothy ('the Demi') *20*, 62, 83, 84
Rees, Juliet (née Gowan) **60**, 72, 85
Rich, Cynthia (née Davies) *74*, *74*
Rich, Tessa *74*
Rich, Zaria *74*
Richards, Gillian (née Taylor) 109
Richmond, Diana (née Galbraith) 34, 84
Rider, Geri (née Woodrow) **78**
Ridler, Anne 6, 16, 37, 82
Rigall, Camilla (née Belloc-Lowndes) **98**
Riley, Bridget 117
Rippon, Miss 121, 122
Risoe, Paul 87, 117, **141–43**, *143*
Ritchie, Katherine 158
Roberts, Mrs 139
Robertson, Dr 47
Rogers, Diane 118
Rowntree, Jean 34, 43, 49, 121
Rucker, Ann 54
Rucker, Elizabeth 54
Russell, Alicia (née Eustace) 30, 36, 40, **41**
Russell, Kit 98
Rylance, Georgina 69

Sackville-West, Jacobine (née Menzies Wilson) **45**, 68
Samuels, Miss 77
Sanderson, Brenda 49, 51
Sandford, Catherine (née Hunt) 19
Schanche, Susan (née Gaddum) 47, 86
Seamark, Sarah (née Fogg-Elliot) 164
Selby, Trevor *86*, 87, 88, 116, 142–143, *143*,*159*
Sellar, Mary (née Norman) **38**
Sharwood Smith, Mr 48, *49*
Shaw, Frank 97
Sidebottom, Albert 87, *88*, 98, *106*, 142–143, *143*
Sidebottom, Barbara 98, 106
Silk, Dennis 117–18
Sinclair, Helen 74

Sinclair, Susan (née Davies) **74**, *74*, 163
Slemeck, Clare 164
Slemeck, Nicola 164
Slemeck, Diana (née Williamson-Napier) 164
Sliwka, Stasio 90
Smallwood, Linda 146
Smith, Tessa (née Kempton) 72
Smith, Miss (history) 75
Smith, Miss (Latin) 121
Spalding, Miss 49, 54
'Spees', The 48–49, 54
Spence, Ohmar 125
Steel, Anthea (née Wilson) 86
Steel, Christopher 86
Stevenson, Rebecca **103**
Stewart Sybil 7
Strange, Doreen *160*, 161
Street, Josephine (née Dane) **48**
Sykes, Deaconess ('Deaky') 67, 73

Tahourdin, Jane (née Haughton) **99**
Tasartey, Mlle ('Tass') 71
Taylor, Cynthia (née Acland) **50**
Taylor, Carolyn (née Medley) 67
Thomson, Patience (née Bragg) 121–22
Travers, Dulcie 14
Tredgold, Rosemary (née Walker) 46
Trumble, Jill 117, 131
Tucker, Vivien (née Forestier-Walker) **80**
Tyrrell, James 105

Verdon-Roe, Katrina 142

Walker, Jennifer **61**
Walker, Josephine (née Holmes) 62, 69
Wallace, Delicia (née Curtis) 34
Warnock, Baroness 97, 128
Watson, Ian 125
Webb, Janice 160, *161*
Wells, Hatty 146
West, Dr 47
Wheaton, Judith *104*, 110, 148, 159
Wheen, Natalie 157
White, Bob 118
White, Evelyn 123
Whittaker, Alice 142
Wilde, Eric 116
Wilkinson, Jack 90
Williams, Monica 158, 161
Willis, Dorothy 6, *10*, 28, 34, 37
Willis, Hilary 14
Willis, Janet 10
Willis, Olive *passim*
Willis Fleming, Rachel (née Hollins) **103**
Wilson, Pamela 17, 19, *73*, 74, 77, 78, 79, 80, 165
Wilson, 'Tig' 80
Wood, Cynthia (née Boot) 33
Wood, Joanna 125
Woodbridge, Rosey (née Handley) **71**
Woodhouse, Sally (née Haggard) 80, 108
Woodroffe, Sue (née Farrer) 55
Wordsworth, Elizabeth 10
Worth, Emily (née Knapp-Fisher) **159**
Wotherspoon, Avril (née Edwards) **50**

Wyld, Janet (née Davies) 68
Wyman, Libby *144*

Young, Mary 50, 63, 76, 160
Young, Elizabeth ('M E') **50**

Topics

This index includes topics discussed in chapter 5 as well as in the green-shaded boxes.

Academic life 1979–2004 128–31

Birthdays 101

Channelling energies 145–47
Chapel 32–33
Children's week 158

Dining Room painting 34
Dogs and other pets 16–17
Downe House Seniors' Association 163
Drama 68–69

Evolution of boarding, The 132–35

Fifth Form leaving dares 102
French Project, The 148–51

Generations and links 164–65
Giant's Stride, The 72

Hair washing 64

Jaws 19
Jennifer Gosse 156–57
Junior School, The 136–40

Meals and food 40–41
Medical matters 46–47
Miss Nickel 15
Music 82–90

Painting and singing at Downe 141–43

Science and other academic development 120–25
Shooting 36
Sleeping arrangements 39
Sport 108–12
Support staff 160–61

There's a man in the house! 106

Uniform 22–25

VE Day remembered fifty years on 55

Wartime memories 52–55
Weekends 42–43
Wider horizons and the French Project 148–51